ROUTLEDGE LIBRARY EDITIONS:
LANGUAGE AND LITERATURE OF THE
MIDDLE EAST

Volume 3

THE ARABIC LINGUISTIC TRADITION

THE ARABIC LINGUISTIC TRADITION

G. BOHAS, J.-P. GUILLAUME,
D.E. KOULOUGHLI

Routledge
Taylor & Francis Group
LONDON AND NEW YORK

First published in 1990 by Routledge

This edition first published in 2017
by Routledge
2 Park Square, Milton Park, Abingdon, Oxon OX14 4RN

and by Routledge
711 Third Avenue, New York, NY 10017

Routledge is an imprint of the Taylor & Francis Group, an informa business

British Library Cataloguing in Publication Data
A catalogue record for this book is available from the British Library

ISBN: 978-1-138-68297-9 (Set)
ISBN: 978-1-315-45973-8 (Set) (ebk)
ISBN: 978-1-138-69903-8 (Volume 3) (hbk)
ISBN: 978-1-138-69904-5 (Volume 3) (pbk)
ISBN: 978-1-315-51277-8 (Volume 3) (ebk)

Publisher's Note
The publisher has gone to great lengths to ensure the quality of this reprint but points out that some imperfections in the original copies may be apparent.

Disclaimer
The publisher has made every effort to trace copyright holders and would welcome correspondence from those they have been unable to trace.

THE ARABIC LINGUISTIC TRADITION

G. Bohas, J.-P. Guillaume, D.E. Kouloughli

ROUTLEDGE

London and New York

First published 1990
by Routledge
11 New Fetter Lane, London EC4P 4EE

Simultaneously published in the USA and Canada
by Routledge
a division of Routledge, Chapman and Hall, Inc.
29 West 35th Street, New York, NY 10001

Typeset by Columns of Reading
Printed in Great Britain by
Biddles Ltd, Guildford

British Library Cataloguing in Publication Data
Bohas, Georges
The Arabic linguistic tradition. – (Arabic thought
and culture)
1. Arabic language. Linguistics, history
I. Title II. Guillaume, Jean-Patrick III.
Kouloughli, Djamel Eddin IV. Series
492′.7

Library of Congress Cataloging in Publication Data
Bohas, Georges.
The Arabic linguistic tradition / G. Bohas, J.-P. Guillaume, D.E.
Kouloughli.
p. cm. – (Arabic thought and culture)
Includes bibliographical references.
1. Linguistics – Arab countries – History. 2. Arabic language –
Grammar – History. I. Guillaume, Jean-Patrick. II. Kouloughli,
D. E. (Djamel Eddine), 1947– . III. Title. IV. Series.
P81.A65B64 1990
410′.917′5927—dc20 89–24088

ISBN 0–415–01904–4

CONTENTS

Preface vii

Transcription system x

1 GENERAL INTRODUCTION 1

The Growth of the Arabic Linguistic Tradition: a Historical Survey; Early grammatical thinking to the end of the second/eighth century; From Sībawayhi to al-Mubarrad; The codification of grammar in the fourth/tenth century; Maturity and decline (fifth/eleventh–tenth/fifteenth centuries). 1

Facts, Rules, and Arguments; Data; The integrative logic of *qiyās*; Grammar and reality 17

2 SĪBAWAYHI'S *KITĀB*: AN ENUNCIATIVE APPROACH TO SYNTAX 31

Problems and Hypotheses; Interpreting the *Kitāb*; The enunciative hypothesis. 33

Predication and Enunciation: Sībawayhi's Theory of the Utterance 42

3 THE CANONICAL THEORY OF GRAMMAR: SYNTAX (*NAḤW*) 49

Basic Concepts; Parts of speech; *I'rāb* and *binā'*; Sentence and utterance. 50

The Theory of Government; General principles; The governing operators; Abstractness in the theory of government. 57

Government and Predication; The two models; Two models or just one? 64

4 THE CANONICAL THEORY OF GRAMMAR: MORPHOLOGY, PHONOLOGY, AND PHONETICS (*TAṢRĪF*) 73
Morphology; Verbal morphology; Derived nominal morphology. 74
Phonology; Substitution (*badal*); Erasure (*ḥaḏf*); Mutation (*qalb*); Transfer (*naql*); Gemination (*idġām*); The late phonological processes. 76
Phonetics; The phonetics of the grammarians; The phonetics of the reciters; The phonetics of the physiologists. *Notes* 93

5 MAJOR TRENDS IN THE STUDY OF TEXTS 100
Literary Criticism. 100
*'Greek' Rhetoric (*Xaṭāba*).* 104
The Foundations of Jurisprudence. 109
*Arabo-Islamic Rhetoric (*Balāġa*)* 113

6 RHETORIC AND GRAMMATICAL SEMANTICS 118
The General Organization of Grammatical Semantics. 119
Some Basic Tenets. 121
Utterance Analysis. 122
Types of Predications. 125
General Operations on Nominals. 127
Informative Predication. 128
Performative Predication. 130
The Scope of Predications. 131
Inter-utterance Relationships. 133
Proper and Figurative Meaning 135

7 METRICS 137
Preliminaries. 137
Observations. 140
The Xalīlian Circles. 141
The Ziḥāfāt. 145
Overgeneration in the Xalīlian System. 149
The Orientalists and the Xalīlian System 150

Bibliography; A Selection 152
References; Primary Sources; Secondary Sources 154
Indexes 159

PREFACE[1]

The corpus of Arabic linguistics constitutes, unquestionably, one of the major linguistic traditions in the world, together with the Indian and Greek ones. It is consequently obvious that the very limited amount of space devoted to the Arab grammarians in the main histories of linguistics (e.g. Robins, 1967) is quite out of proportion to the real importance of this tradition. On the other hand, if the linguists, the historians of grammatical theories, and the public interested in Islamic culture have not appreciated just how interesting it is, that is obviously because Arabists failed to make them understand it. Furthermore, in order to do that, it would have been necessary for these scholars to take some interest in the knowledge of the language and in the specialized literature, approaching those texts as technical treatises and therefore something intelligible, and not like an impenetrable and abstruse farrago, and also to take the trouble to acquire the linguistic and conceptual means of understanding them before claiming to have grasped the conception of the Arab grammarians about some point or other.

The present work aims to give an overall view of the sciences of language in the Arabic culture. For this purpose it is based on the analytical works carried out by the three authors, starting from 1975.[2] The main ideas which have guided these works can be summed up in the following points:

1 The Arab grammarians' texts constitute an indispensable source for any description of Arabic, not only by dint of the facts which they relate, but also through the explanations of them which they give.

2 The theory of the Arab grammarians, aside from any comparative work on the sources and influences, constitutes a subject worthy of study in itself. Work on the sources (Indian and Greek) and the influences (Aristotelian logic, Islamic law, or Stoic grammar) constitutes a different field: there should be no question of confusing them. Furthermore, in respect of the sources, the question is, in our opinion, to know whether there was a borrowing of theoretical framework and not to know whether Arabic grammar owes something or does not owe anything at all to neighbouring cultures. Indeed, what constitutes the unity and specific nature of a discipline is not whether it has invented notions and terminology *ex nihilo* and completely without any analogue, but whether it has its own way of defining concepts and of organizing them and its own way of problematizing the relationship between these concepts and the observable data. This comparison of paradigm obviously necessitates a very technical and precise study of the discipline in question, not just a mere tracing of possible 'sources'.

3 The Arabic linguistic texts being technical, it follows that they must be read with a technical approach, which implies that the reader should have at his or her disposal adequate conceptual tools, and should use the same precise scientific method and the same attention to detail which would be required when analysing contemporary linguistic texts. Finally, we have from the beginning adopted the point of view expressed thus by Auroux (1986:17): 'We are henceforward in a period when the work of the historian of linguistic theories is more about a precise description of the theories than about the history of ideas.' Furthermore, could one, today, consider proceeding otherwise if one were undertaking the study of the other technical branches of the Islamic field, such as mathematics or law?

4 In so far as it is a matter of making the linguistic theories of the Arabs understandable to the contemporary reader, having recourse to one or another linguistic theory elaborated during the last hundred years could only be considered a heuristic method, making it possible to show how fundamentally different theories can explain the same facts and, perhaps, to make a parallel regarding the methods and manners of argumentation. For us, modern linguistic theories are merely instruments with which to

'interrogate' the Arabic texts in order to be able to make the theories developed in them explicit. It is by no means our intention to show that the methods that they embody can be explained in terms of one or another of the modern theories, for it seems obvious to us that such an 'explanation' would be pointless in so far as it would not teach us anything about anything.

That the Arabic linguistic texts, like the product of all human activity, must be placed in their historic and social context, and that the effect of this context must be recognized, is something that no one would think of contesting. And so it is by outlining this context, or at least what can be known about it at the present moment, that we will begin this book.

NOTES

1 Two abbreviations will be used all over the book: ALT for 'Arabic Linguistic Tradition', and AG for 'Arabic Grammarians'. Wherever relevant, dates will be given in pairs separated by an oblique, first according to the Muslim era (AH) and second according to the Christian era (AD).

2 Many people have helped us, through their teachings, writings, or oral communications: the list would be long, but S. Barakāt in Damascus, K. Versteegh, M. Carter, and S. Auroux deserve a special mention. We also wish to thank H. Anderson for his help in translating some of the chapters into English. Finally we thank the Département de Recherche Linguistique of Paris-7 University and particularly Professor A. Culioli for the moral and material help with which we have constantly been provided.

TRANSCRIPTION SYSTEM

ʼ	ء	ẓ	ظ
b	ب	ʻ	ع
t	ت	ḡ	غ
ṯ	ث	f	ف
ǧ	ج	q	ق
ḥ	ح	k	ک
x	خ	l	ل
d	د	m	م
ḏ	ذ	n	ن
r	ر	h	ه
z	ز	w	و
s	س	y	ي
š	ش		
ṣ	ص	ā	ـَا
ḍ	ض	ū	ـُو
ṭ	ط	ī	ـِي

1

GENERAL INTRODUCTION

THE GROWTH OF THE ARABIC LINGUISTIC TRADITION: A HISTORICAL SURVEY

Early grammatical thinking to the end of the second/eighth century

As is generally well known, the first grammatical treatise of unquestionable authenticity is Sībawayhi's *Kitāb* (this title means 'The Book' or 'Sībawayhi's Book'). This work, whose author died in or about 177/798, is most probably the first attempt at a comprehensive and systematic description of the Arabic language at every level (phonetics, phonology, morphology, syntax, and semantics). In spite of the great originality of its approach, notably in syntax (see Chapter 2), the breadth of its scope and the depth of its insights clearly point to at least some kind of pre-existent reflection on grammar, even if this reflection had perhaps not yet crystallized into an autonomous discipline.

According to medieval Arabic sources, grammar was first 'invented' by Abū l-Aswad al-Du'alī (d. 69/688?) on the basis of a 'personnal communication' (as we would call it nowadays) by ʿAlī ibn Abī Ṭālib (d. 40/660), the Prophet's cousin and son-in-law. Although it is still accepted by some Arabists (e.g. Mubārak, 1974: 10–37), this account is generally discarded as legend. Another opinion associates, perhaps more plausibly, the emergence of grammar with ʿAbd Allāh ibn Abī Isḥāq (d. 117/734), who is said to have 'divided grammar and measured it', *farraʿa al-naḥwa wa-qāsa-hu* (Abū l-Ṭayyib, *Marātib*: 12; see Fleisch, 1961: 27; Talmon, 1986), which points to an attempt at a systematical classification of grammatical facts and at building general rules by way of abstract reasoning (*qiyās*, see next section).

But the important thing is perhaps not so much to discuss the claims of the different candidates to the title of first Arabic grammarian, than to have a reasonably clear picture of the kind of discussions in which the first manifestations of grammatical thought appeared, as the nature of these discussions had an enduring formative influence on the approach and problems of the later tradition. All these discussions, in fact, can be related to a single, major event: the shift of Arabic from a mainly oral language, specific to an ethnically (more or less) homogeneous community of 'native' speakers, to a language adapted to a basically written use by an elite of mixed ethnic backgrounds, within a richer and more complex cultural framework.

The first kind of discussion, and perhaps the most ancient, is related to the recension of the Qur'ān and its fixation for ritual recitation. Most of the figures associated with the early developments of grammar and philology are mentioned in connection with the branch of knowledge technically called *qirā'āt* ('readings' or 'recitations', i.e. of the Qur'ān), the purpose of which was to sift the many variant readings which were compatible with the ancient Arabic script in which the oldest copies of the holy text were written. These variants, which seldom carried important differences of meaning, appeared mostly at the morpho-phonological and morpho-syntactical levels. Although it was universally admitted that more than one reading could legitimately exist for a given verse, it was also considered necessary to distinguish between 'acceptable' and 'unacceptable' readings, and, among the former, between 'current' and 'rare' ones. The basic criterion was, apart from the reliability of the transmitters, the conformity to the 'speech of the Arabs', that is the specific linguistic usage of the Beduins of Central Arabia, in the pre-Islamic and early Islamic period.

The second kind of discussion is related to the collection and criticism of ancient poetry, which played perhaps a more decisive and enduring part in the constitution of the philological sciences. The problems which confronted the scholars engaged in this work were basically identical with those relating to the *qirā'āt*, but were considerably more complex. On the one hand, ancient poetry provided scholars with an infinitely vaster and more diversified sample of *kalām al-ʿArab* than the Qur'ān did; poetry made greater use of specialized vocabulary, rare words, difficult constructions, tribal dialectalisms, and so forth. On the other hand, the transmitters of poetry seem to have been, on the whole, much less careful than the transmitters of the Qur'ān. As commonly happens within oral traditions, they tended, more or less consciously, to modify the poems as they transmitted them; some would even interpolate lines of their own in some piece of verse by an older poet, or forge whole pieces outright. The extensive scope and complexity of the problems entailed by this situation goes towards explaining why the body of 'philological sciences' (*'ulūm al-'Arabiyya*, literally 'sciences of Arabity'), which formed the context in which grammar first grew, seems to be mainly focussed on the poetic heritage of ancient Arabia, as it comprised, besides grammar proper (*naḥw*), lexicography (*'ilm al-luġa*), a specialized field of which was devoted to 'rare' words (*ġarīb*), metrics (*'ilm al-'arūḍ*), and even the knowledge of the famous battles and tribal wars of the ancient Arabs (*ayyām al-'Arab*), and of their genealogies (*'ilm al-ansāb*). These two last branches of knowledge were necessary in order to understand the recondite allusions to tribal feuds and alliances found in the most characteristic kind of ancient poetry.

The third formative factor is the reform initiated by the Umayyad caliph 'Abd al-Malik ibn Marwān (reigned 65/685–86/705), by which Arabic became the sole administrative language of the Islamic empire. Although we still lack a comprehensive study of the changes that such a reform entailed in the technical and cultural practices associated with language, they cannot but have been quite extensive and, in many ways, decisive. In the long term, their effects were enhanced by the fact that the 'scribes' (*kuttāb*), besides their specific function as administrators, were soon to give the tone to most aspects of classical Islamic high culture. By accepting (probably after some resistance, bureaucratic circles being what they are) that the 'speech of distinguished people' (*kalām al-xawāṣṣ*) had to conform with what was most representative of *kalām al-'Arab*, as opposed to the 'degraded' vernacular spoken by the populace, they certainly contributed to the general social relevance of grammatical and philological studies.

Such was, then, the context in which appeared the first manifestations of grammatical thought. By the end of the second/eighth century, it was already in a state of considerable advancement and, in some fields, had even evolved its definitive forms. Such was the case of phonetics and metrics, which were codified by al-Xalīl (d. 175/791), Sībawayhi's teacher. Al-Xalīl is also credited with having devised the basic principles of lexicography in his *Kitāb al-ʿAyn*, the first Arabic dictionary. As for morpho-phonology (*taṣrīf*) and syntax (*naḥw* proper), even if their definitive, canonical form would not be codified until the fourth/tenth century, they had already evolved some of their basic concepts and devices.

Many Arabists have stressed the remarkably swift pace at which the Arabic grammatical tradition had, in so short a period, developed into a complex and sophisticated set of concepts and procedures. According to them, such a precocity can only be accounted for by the effect of some extraneous influence. This influence has been variously identified with Aristotelian logic (Merx, 1889), Islamic law (Carter, 1968 and 1972), or Stoic grammar (Versteegh, 1977). Such a variety of hypotheses sufficiently indicates that no one of them is, in fact, completely satisfying; on the other hand, none can be completely discarded, even if the actual evidence adduced by their respective authors is, to our minds, often unconvincing (that of Merx is, to put it frankly, quite fanciful). In fact, their main failing is that they try to explain the whole of the grammatical tradition in terms of one single factor, which is unnecessary (whatever their respective authors claim to the contrary, these hypotheses are not mutually incompatible), and, indeed, runs counter to the most currently accepted methodology of historical studies. In our opinion, at least, the important thing is that, whatever its model or models can have been, the Arabic tradition developed into something quite different and original; a point on which, moreover, everybody more or less agrees.

From Sībawayhi to al-Mubarrad

Although Sībawayhi's and al-Xalīl's contribution to the development of the grammatical tradition was in many ways decisive, it did not result in the constitution of a definitive canonical model for grammatical theory. Actually, such a model was not evolved until the first decade of the fourth/tenth century, its first expression being the *Kitāb al-Uṣūl* by Ibn al-Sarrāǧ (d. 316/928). The importance of this event has for a long time been underestimated, for many reasons (among others, the fact that the

Kitāb al-Uṣūl was not published until quite recently), and the accepted idea has been that Sībawayhi had, in fact, laid down the basic rules and methods of grammar, while the later grammarians' contribution consisted only in expounding his theory in a more explicit and systematic form, or in finding new applications for it. Such a linear conception of the history of the grammatical tradition led, in fact, to many misrepresentations and false problems.

In the next chapter, we shall try to show that Sībawayhi's syntactic system is, on the whole, founded on a quite different approach from that of the classical grammarians. But if, in originality and perception, the *Kitāb* certainly stands alone among the grammatical products of its period, even a perfunctory examination of the few treatises surviving from before the fourth/tenth century shows that they exhibit some common traits which distinguish them collectively from the products of later periods. The most obvious of these is perhaps their extreme heterogeneity in scope, in approach, and even in terminology, together with a strong dependency on what one could call a 'philological' outlook. The primary interest of the earlier grammarians is not (as it will be for their successors) in explicitly laying down general rules and principles in order to classify and analyse linguistic facts; it is rather in examining and discussing isolated, specific data, especially when these data exhibit some kind of deviance from the most general behaviour of the class to which they belong. It is, for instance, typical of this approach that al-Mubarrad (d. 285/898), in his *Muqtaḍab*, devotes a whole chapter to the irregular plural of *qaws* ('bow') *qisiyy*, this chapter being somewhat longer than the one in which he discusses the much more general and, we should feel, important problem of the assignation of the nominative to the subject of the verbal phrase (*Muqtaḍab*, I: 8–9 and 39–41, respectively). This kind of approach, in which facts of different nature and rules of different degree of generality are put together in what seems a haphazard order, is also quite perceptible in the two other main grammatical works of the period, the *Ma'ānī l-Qur'ān* by al-Farrā' (d. 207/822), who was in his time the leader of the so-called 'Kūfan' school (see below, pp. 6–8), and a shorter work bearing the same title by al-Axfaš al-Awsaṭ (d. 221/835), a disciple of Sībawayhi. In these two works, which are grammatical and philological commentaries on the Qur'ān, the order and nature of the problems discussed are more or less governed by the order in which they appear in the text. They show a wide range of interests, but with a stress on lexicology and morpho-phonology, syntax (with the exception of morpho-syntax) receiving a more perfunctory treatment. In fact, it seems that, throughout this period, Sībawayhi was the only grammarian to show a deep and systematic interest in the field of syntax.

This lack of canonical theoretical model does not mean, of course, that grammar was still in a 'pre-theoretical' state. As a matter of fact, grammarians systematically used abstract, general rules and principles when analysing and discussing individual facts but these rules and principles were never formally stated, rather, they were taken for granted, as if they were a matter of current knowledge. To put it differently: one could say that they formed a kind of general intuitive background in the light of which the grammarians approached linguistic data: it only became consciously acknowledged when some kind of fact occurred which was felt to need explanation, for instance when *qaws*, instead of forming a regular plural, *quwūs* (as, for instance, *qalb/qulūb*), forms an irregular one, *qisiyy*; this naturally implies that one has, somewhere in the background, a theory about what the regular plural for this class of nouns should be.

On the other hand, the informal and intuitive nature of the theoretical framework offered a wide scope for individual improvization and interpretation; as long as the basic principles and rules which governed grammatical analysis were not explicitly and systematically defined, even minimally compatible solutions to a given problem could coexist and still be considered as equally legitimate, or indeed substantially equivalent. This property of the grammatical theory in this period is crucial in order to form a clear picture of a much-discussed point of historiography: the rivalry between the Baṣran and Kūfan 'schools' of grammar. In fact, many of the difficulties relating to this problem arise, in our opinion, from an inadequate appreciation of the change that intervened in the grammatical tradition when the canonical model was finally evolved.

Philological and grammatical studies first appeared in Baṣra and Kūfa, the two main cities of lower Iraq, which were the principal centres of learning in early Islam, until they were supplanted by Baghdad about the middle of the third/ninth century. In this sense, one can speak of a Baṣran and a Kūfan 'school' of grammar, but one should keep in mind that a 'school' (*maḏhab*) in classical Islam refers not so much to a specific body of doctrine as to a channel of transmission of knowledge, by personal contact between master and pupil (there was no other legitimate access to knowledge); on such bases, Zellig Harris and Noam Chomsky would be considered as belonging to the same 'school', as the latter was, for some time, the pupil of the former, quite independently of their theoretical divergence. Of course, grammarians of the same 'school' could have in common some tenets which distinguished them from others, but these tenets did not necessarily have deep theoretical implications. In fact, the divergences between grammarians of Baṣra and of Kūfa in the pre-canonical period were simply a particular aspect of the general situation of grammar, where the implicit and informal character of the theory made for the coexistence of several potentially conflicting solutions or analyses for the same problem.

In fact, it is even quite possible, as Fleisch (1961) suggests, that the theme of the conflict between the two schools was actually invented after the fact, as a kind of historical justification for the personal rivalry between al-Mubarrad (d. 285/898), the leader of the 'Baṣrans', and Ṯaʿlab (d. 291/904), his 'Kūfan' counterpart, when they met in Baghdad. But the important thing is that, when the canonical model was evolved, a generation later, by al-Mubarrad's disciples, they naturally gave it the 'Baṣran' label. Now, this model, because of its explicit and systematic character, was naturally more constrained than the former, which had been, in fact, common to Baṣran and Kūfan grammarians alike. In consequence, many views which had hitherto seemed acceptable and legitimate, now appeared incompatible with the new model. An efficient way to make them harmless was to attribute them to the 'Kūfan school', which had by then become virtually extinct. From this point on, there was a basic asymmetry between allegedly Baṣran and Kūfan material: whereas the Baṣran views all fell together within a systematic, organized system, the Kūfan, on the contrary, gave the impression of being a haphazard collection of views on points of detail, from which it seems quite difficult to reconstruct any kind of coherent system. The obvious reason is, of course, that they were never meant to have any coherence. A failure to recognize this most crucial point has often misled Arabists into characterizing the Kūfan grammarians as staunch defenders of linguistic 'usage' as based on 'transmitted' data (*samāʿ*), while the Baṣrans were described as partisans of 'analogy' (*qiyās*) and of a 'rationalization' of language. In so far as they mean anything, such statements relate not to any actual historical school or tendency within the Arabic tradition, but only the 'official' interpretation concocted by later grammarians (who considered, anyway, that both *samāʿ* and *qiyās* were indissociable components of any grammatical theory). This does not mean, of course, that the literature devoted to the 'disputed questions' between the two schools should be ignored as mere irrelevant legend; on the contrary, all the discussions which took place within the grammatical tradition are important, as they can often shed significant light on far-reaching theoretical issues. On the other hand, it would be misleading to accept this kind of material as relating to a single, historically datable controversy, and to try accordingly to reconstruct from it both 'doctrines' as they were supposed to exist in this particular period.

The codification of grammar in the fourth/tenth century

As we said above, the last years of the third/ninth century were characterized, as far as grammar is concerned, by the rivalry between al-Mubarrad and Ṯaʿlab. The final triumph of the former brought about an enduring homogenization of grammatical circles: for one century, at least, all the important grammarians would be either al-Mubarrad's disciples, or his disciples' disciples. Of course, this did not prevent a certain amount of personal rivalry and back-biting, but it nevertheless contributed to grammarians' stronger sense of commitment to common norms and expectations, embodied in an informal but influential grammatical 'establishment'. This basic cohesion was further enhanced by the fact that grammatical and philological studies, which had been, up to this period, confined to small circles of specialists, found themselves in contact, for the first time, with a wider cultural context, in terms of which the tradition had to define its specific status and function.

One of the most important characteristics of this context was the part played in it by the Hellenic philosophical tradition (*falsafa*), which was then at the apex of its public influence in Islamic lands, and more or less overtly aimed at cultural hegemony. This new factor put the grammarians, taken collectively, in a difficult predicament. On one hand, *falsafa* could afford them much intellectual stimulation, on many counts: it went for new, higher standards and expectations about what a scientific discipline should be, while offering new opportunities for meeting these standards; moreover, it had evolved its own system for the analysis of utterances, logic, which could provide grammarians with fresh insights on the nature of language, together with new concepts and techniques from which they could benefit in their own field.

But, on the other hand, the difficulty was in accepting the general premises underlying *falsafa*'s interest in language. For the philosopher, language was only relevant as a vehicle for universal truths, which were measured by logic, according to principles which were, naturally, universal, that is language-independent. Individual idioms, such as Arabic or Greek or Persian were only the contingent, inessential forms in which universal truths were expressed. Grammar, which studied the specific properties of these idioms (as opposed to the universal ones), was necessarily confined to the outward, inessential 'form' (*lafẓ*) of utterances, while only logic could examine their significant, universal 'meaning' (*maʿnā*). Within these limits, philosophers were quite ready to accept grammar as a science of a kind, as they accepted such specifically Islamic disciplines as law and theology; but, if the specialists of these sciences could be considered as belonging to the elite relatively to their several communities, the only real elite in the 'absolute', universal meaning, were the philosophers.

Grammarians, then, could not go too far in accepting what *falsafa* could offer them without accepting, by the same token, not only an important downgrading of their own social status to that of a 'provincial' kind of elite compared with philosophers, but also a drastic re-evaluation of all the cultural values which made their discipline relevant. If, as the philosophers claimed, *kalām al-ʿArab* was just a language among others, and rather unsophisticated at that, it followed that all the rich and vast knowledge that generation after generation of grammarians and philologists had collected by patient and minute observation of a comprehensive body of data was just an exercise in myopic pedantry, and that the Arabic tribal tradition on which this knowledge was founded, far from being relevant to any kind of universalistic high culture, was only a piece of local folklore.

The grammarians' response to this predicament took two different but complementary forms. On one hand, an effort was made to codify grammar into a systematic descriptive theory, based upon explicit general rules and principles, so that every particular class of facts was accurately provided for in its proper rank and place; this aspect of the grammarians' work is called, in contemporary texts, the *uṣūl*, the 'foundations'. On the other hand, grammarians attempted to clarify in a way both meaningful and attractive for contemporary readers (especially those who had leanings towards *falsafa*) some of the deep insights which informed their own view of *kalām al-ʿArab*, in order to show that their discipline had not only practical uses, but could open up whole realms of high speculation. This level of reflection, which until then had not been clearly distinguished from the descriptive level, was usually called the *ʿilal*, the 'causes' or 'explanations'. But, at every level, grammarians, while taking advantage of the epistemological resources offered by the new cultural context, were nevertheless careful to keep within the borders fixed by the tradition. Actually, the most technical level of grammar (i.e. the categories and procedures used in description and analysis of linguistic data), which determined the economy of the system, was practically untouched by 'Greek borrowings'.

As we said above, the *uṣūl* approach was first codified by Ibn al-Sarrāǧ, in his *Kitāb al-Uṣūl*. This treatise, incidentally, was also the first to state the distinction of principle between the *uṣūl* levels and the *ʿilal* level in grammatical analysis. The system devised by Ibn al-Sarrāǧ for the classification of facts and the exposition of problems is based on the principles of 'exhaustive divisions' (*taqāsīm*), which he is said to have borrowed from logic, which he had, for some time, studied with al-Fārābī (d. 339/950), the leading figure of contemporary *falsafa*. But the actual criteria on which these 'divisions' operate belong typically to the grammatical tradition. The first, most general one is founded on the parts of speech, as any given word is necessarily either a noun, or a verb, or a particle. The first main section of the book is accordingly devoted to the noun, which can be either nominative, or accusative, or genitive; if it is nominative it can be either the theme (*mubtadaʾ*) of a nominal sentence, or its predicate (*xabar*), or the subject (*fāʿil*) of a verbal sentence, or the subject substitute when the verb is passive, or because its status is formally assimilated to that of the subject of a verb. The same approach applies to the accusative and the genitive noun, then to the verb, then to the particle.

In such a way, every possible case is theoretically provided for, and its treatment occurs in a predictable place in the treatise. Moreover, the careful system of divisions, subdivisions and sub-subdivisions devised by Ibn al-Sarrāǧ makes the hierarchical relations between grammatical categories and classes of facts immediately visible. It was, certainly, a considerable practical improvement: for any given question, one could, by referring to the relevant section, find at a glance all the data, analyses, and opinions relating to it; moreover, its exact status within the theory was clearly and transparently expressed by its location in the book. But such a seemingly 'technical' readjustment could, in some cases, have important consequences on the theoretical level. For instance, the fact that the subject of the verbal sentence found itself side by side with the theme and the predicate of the nominal sentence within the class of 'nouns affected with the nominative' could focus the attention of the most perceptive grammarians on the underlying generality which accounted for that similarity. This resulted in the upgrading of the concept of predication, which, until then, had remained at most a rather secondary aspect of the grammatical theory. Such a process, already incipient in the *Kitāb al-Uṣūl*, found its logical conclusion in al-Astarābāḏī's audacious rehabilitation of the 'Kūfan' analysis of the nominal sentence (see Chap. 3).

As we said above, the system devised by Ibn al-Sarrāǧ became, with some minor adjustments and/or variants, the general norm for all the later classical treatises. Such acceptance, however, took some time to become effective and, although the *Kitāb al-Uṣūl* certainly influenced many treatises of the period, some of them, however, still exhibit a different way of presenting grammatical facts, nearer to the classification of Sībawayhi's *Kitāb* (but without Sībawayhi's insights).

As for the *ʿilal* approach, it seems to have given rise to rather important literature throughout the period; most of it, however, is no longer (or perhaps not yet) accessible to us, with two exceptions: the *Kiṭab al-Īḍāḥ* by al-Zaǧǧāǧī (d. 340/951) and the *Xaṣā'iṣ* by Ibn Ǧinnī (d. 392/1002). Although these two works are quite different in many ways, they are founded on identical presuppositions: (a) that the grammatical theory evolved by the Arabic tradition is not only able to describe facts as they are, but also to explain why they are so; and (b) that this explanatory power of grammar is a consequence of the pervasive order, harmony and rationality which uniquely characterizes *kalām al-ʿArab*, as opposed to other human idioms. These ideas have often been misunderstood and misrepresented as a piece of local folklore, which could perhaps shed light on the 'Arabic mind' (whatever it is), but was completely irrelevant to any kind of serious, 'scientific' approach to linguistic facts. Such an assessment seems altogether superficial and founded on a rather naive kind of positivism. Actually, the Arabic grammarians' claims on this subject can be considered as the expression, within a specific cultural environment, of what is a necessary postulate for any kind of linguistic or grammatical theory: that a language is not a haphazard collection of unrelated arbitrary facts, but that it forms an ordered whole, or, to use the well-known formula of de Saussure, 'un système où tout se tient'.

But perhaps the expression of this idea which seems to correspond best to the Arabic grammarians' insight is that of Gustave Guillaume, the founder of the psychomechanist school of linguistics: 'Une intuition: que le désordre *apparent* des faits linguistiques recouvre un ordre secret, caché – *merveilleux*' (G. Guillaume, 1973 [1952–3]: 17). Of course, Guillaume's way of understanding this 'order' was quite different from the Arabic grammarians' (it was also different, incidentally, from de Saussure's); but what is important here is that common feeling, or intuition, which seems to create a kind of bond between linguists and grammarians belonging to quite different periods of time and intellectual traditions. This deep sense of wonder, of uncovering deeper and deeper hidden correspondences between apparently unrelated phenomena, of contemplating wider and wider realms of order and harmony, was never better or more significantly expressed, within the Arabic tradition, than in the *Xaṣāʾiṣ*.

This work, which reflects its author's dominant interest in morpho-phonology, can be read at a multiplicity of levels. Written in a formal, ornate style which contrasts with the simpler prose commonly used in technical treatises (whether in grammar or in other disciplines), it evidently aims at conforming with the standards of contemporary 'courtly literature' (*adab*), which was expected to be informative while affording intellectual pleasure and excitement. It is divided into chapters, each one being devoted to a question relating to grammatical methodology or epistemology; in treating every question, Ibn Ǧinnī carefully avoids being systematic or exhaustive (such an approach, smacking of pedantry, was excluded by the rules of the genre), but tries to make his point by examining and discussing a wide range of questions of detail, so that each one of them sheds a particular light on the main question, and helps to build a general picture of it. In so doing, he shows a remarkable virtuosity, spinning the same line of reasoning for page after page while going through a dazzling variety of local arguments and analyses, in the same way that some classical Arabic poets can spin the same basic metaphor or comparison through line after line while always finding new and original ways of expressing it.

At first glance, this display of dialectic fireworks can seem baffling, or even gratuitous; in some cases, Ibn Ǧinnī's reasoning can appear specious or downright sophistic, but a more careful reading shows that this 'baroque' kind of writing is, in itself, deeply significant. If, as Ibn Ǧinnī claims, the pervasive order and harmony that grammarians perceive in *kalām al-ʿArab* is actually an intrinsic property of this language, and if it is not superimposed on the facts by the activity of the grammarians, then the best way to make this order and harmony apparent is to take one's departure from any arbitrary chosen question or class of facts, and to let oneself be guided by the internal logic of the language. By contrast, an approach classifying facts and arguments into rigid categories and subcategories, on the lines of the *Kitāb al-Uṣūl*, would have been much less effective here, as it would have resulted in obscuring what is, for Ibn Ǧinnī, a most fascinating particularity of *kalām al-ʿArab*: that every class of facts is mysteriously connected to all the others, even if some of these connections (those on which didactic grammars are built) are more immediately perceptible, while some others can only be discovered by the shrewdest and most clever specialists.

The *Xaṣā'iṣ* certainly represents the most original and significant treatment of what was, originally, a polemical theme used by Arabic grammarians against Hellenizing philosophers, as clearly appears through the well-known account of the controversy between Abū Bišr and al-Sīrāfī (see Margoliouth, 1905; Mahdī, 1970): namely, that what is most relevant about *kalām al-ʿArab* is not its universal properties (the only aspect of any individual language in which *falsafa* was interested) but its most specific ones. In the following period, the debate seems to have quickly lost its immediacy; *falsafa* gradually disappeared from the public scene, surviving only as a kind of 'underground' intellectual tradition, while many aspects of it (notably logic) found a place within the new Islamic cultural context brought about by the 'Sunni restoration' of the second half of the fifth/eleventh century. But, in this period, *falsafa* had played a crucial part in the development of the grammatical tradition, if perhaps not so much by direct influence than by the challenge it had posed to grammarians and the new standards it had established.

Maturity and decline (fifth/eleventh–tenth/fifteenth centuries)

With the notable exception of text linguistics and grammatical semantics (see chaps 5 and 6), this period saw no radically new development of grammatical theory. Grammarians were primarily concerned with the consolidation and preservation of the advances made by the fourth/tenth-century masters. The canonical framework devised by Ibn al-Sarrāǧ was elaborated upon and improved in many minor ways; some of its implications were worked out and discussed on a more explicit and systematic basis, but its most fundamental premises were never questioned.

Here we have, so to speak, the grammatical tradition at its most traditional, if by that one means a basic sense of continuity, a concern with accumulation and conservation of knowledge more than with invention and eagerness to discover fresh insights. This spirit (which, by the way, pervaded most aspects of the contemporary Islamic civilization, especially those which were expressed in Arabic) is manifest, for instance, in the fact that the most common and, indeed, expected way of expounding the grammatical theory was either to write a commentary (*šarḥ*) on an already existing work, or to compose an epitome (*talxīṣ*) for somebody else to comment upon. Sometimes, even, the same author could write both the epitome and the commentary. This is the case, for instance, with two works by Ibn Hišām (d. 761/1359), the *Šarḥ Qatr al-Nadā* and the *Šarḥ Šaḏarāt al-Ḏahab*. In later periods, commentaries were even written on commentaries; they are usually called *ḥāšiya* ('stuffing'), as opposed to the first-degree commentary, *šarḥ*.

Now, such practices were not completely ignored in earlier periods: in the fourth/tenth century, two commentaries at least were written on the *Kitāb*, one by al-Sīrāfī (d. 368/979) and one by al-Rummānī (d. 384/994), while Ibn Ǧinnī wrote a very short summary of morpho-phonology, the *Taṣrīf al-Mulūkī*, which is mainly known through its commentary by Ibn Yaʿīš (d. 643/1245), the *Šarḥ al-Mulūkī*. But what was new in this later period was that most summaries were written with an express view to being commented, so that, in some cases, they are virtually illegible without a proper commentary. Such is the case, for instance, of the *Alfiyya* by Ibn Mālik (d. 672/1273), a didactic poem of about a thousand verses, which was, perhaps, one of the most often commented summaries in the history of the tradition, together with Ibn Āǧurrūm's *Āǧurrūmiyya*.

The generalization of the (so to speak) epitome-cum-commentary system naturally reinforced the homogeneity of the tradition. Of course, the commentator could always express his disagreement on some point or another with the author upon whom he commented, but then, as the general system became more and more elaborate, all the possible solutions to a given problem were eventually worked out, together with the arguments for and against every solution, so the only way one could disagree with somebody on some point was to accept somebody else's position on this point. Moreover, the most fundamental postulates of the theory (e.g. that there are three parts of speech, or that the purpose of case endings is to express the different meanings which can affect a noun) were considered to be agreed upon once and for all, and were not to be questioned.

These constraints oriented the creativity of the grammarians into new channels. The writing of grammar was, in this period, brought to a hitherto unknown degree of formal perfection. Authors of epitomes were at great pains to find the most exact and precise wording for definitions and general rules, making implicit provisos for every possible objection or counterexample, while taking care to avoid redundancy, which would immediately attract criticism. Commentators analysed these formulations in the most careful way, showing how they covered all relevant data and only relevant data, or else pointed to their inconsistencies and/or redundancies. At every step of the reasoning, all conceivable objections were thoroughly and seriously discussed, even those which seem to us most naive or irrelevant. On the other hand, many important data and/or discussions were only referred to through brief allusions, as the author took for granted that the reader was already familiar with them.

The treatises written in this period can be considered, in a way, as the most representative expressions of the tradition. Some of them, such as the *Šarḥ al-Mufaṣṣal* by Ibn Yaʿīš, the *Šarḥ al-Kāfiya* by al-Astarābāḏī (d. 686/1287), the *Muḡnī l-Labīb* by Ibn Hišām, the commentaries on the *Alfiyya* by Ibn ʿAqīl (d. 769/1367), Ibn Hišām, and al-Ašmūnī (d. 900/1494), the *Hamʿ al-Hawāmiʿ Šarḥ Ǧamʿ al-Ǧawāmiʿ* by al-Suyūṭī (d. 911/1505), are still used as standard textbooks for the teaching of traditional grammar at university level in Arabic and Muslim countries, and certainly offer the most accessible introduction to the tradition taken as a whole. For this reason, they are quite often referred to by linguists engaged in research on Standard Arabic, as they contain the most comprehensive and accurate description of the language available to this day.

At first glance, these works can give an impression of tedious repetition. Such an impression is, however, not only inaccurate but seriously misleading. One of the characteristics of the theory evolved by the Arabic tradition is its extreme coherence and systematicity, so that the treatment of a given question is, to a wide extent, pre-determined by a multiplicity of decisions taken at other points of the theory, these points being often quite distant from the original question, and apparently quite unrelated to it. But then all such connections are not explicitly stated by any single treatise; on the other hand, different treatises can very often shed different lights on the same question, by suggesting different connections. It follows that the best way to get an accurate idea of the treatment of any question in the Arabic tradition is by reading the chapters devoted to it in a number of treatises; in most cases, the difficulties raised by an author can be solved by a chance remark passed by another. If one approaches the texts in such a way, one very quickly realizes that they are not repetitive, but cumulative.

Al-Suyūṭī (d. 911/1505) was the last Arabic grammarian of note. Although his works are characterized by a pervasively conservative spirit, he still preserves the basic theoretical insights which informed the classical theory. After him, grammatical theory gradually degenerated into a set of prescriptive recipes, to which some dry strips of dead theory still adhered. The nineteenth-century *Nahḍa*, in the name of simplification and 'common sense', only kept the recipes, cutting them completely from their theoretical roots. This degenerated version of the tradition is, to this day, the basis for teaching grammars used in most Arabic countries.

FACTS, RULES, AND ARGUMENTS

While the main part of the written output within the Arabic linguistic tradition consists of descriptive treatises, a few works are devoted to methodological and epistemological questions relating to grammatical analysis. Besides the two surviving fourth/tenth-century *ʿilal* treatises that we have already mentioned, al-Zaǧǧāǧī's *Īḍāḥ* and Ibn Ǧinnī's *Xaṣā'iṣ*, one should also mention two later works, Abū l-Barakāt al-Anbārī's *Lumaʿ al-Adilla* and al-Suyūṭī's *Iqtirāḥ*; these two short books belong to what was then called *uṣūl al-naḥw* ('foundations of grammar'). It should be noted that this expression has a quite different meaning from what the fourth/tenth-century grammarians intended by *uṣūl*, namely, the didactic–descriptive level of grammar, as opposed to theoretical speculation (*ʿilal*). In its later usage, *uṣūl al-naḥw* is actually a calque on *uṣūl al-fiqh* ('foundations of jurisprudence'), that is the autonomous discipline which studied the abstract form of juridical prescriptions and reasoning, independent of their actual positive contents.

Although the information collected from these works cannot be considered as a satisfactory equivalent for a real, in-depth epistemological study of the Arabic linguistic sciences, which is still lacking, we felt that on many points it could help in forming a clearer picture of some basic attitudes common to the whole tradition, even if they are perhaps more self-conscious and explicit in the classical periods.

Data

The grammatical tradition was confronted by two distinct kinds of problem relating to linguistic data. The first was to distinguish on clear, explicit criteria what could and could not be considered as 'authoritative' (*ḥuǧǧa*) data, i.e. authentically representative of the actual use of the original Arabs. The second was concerned with classifying data according to their degree of relevance to linguistic analysis, or (but from the Arabic grammarians' point of view it amounts to the same thing) their status within the general system of the language.

The first kind of problem is often referred to in the texts by the expression *naql al-luġa* ('transmission of the data'), since the standard way of assessing the authenticity (and, by way of consequence, the authoritativeness) of information within Classical Islamic thought was to examine the circumstances in which it had been transmitted from its original source. But then, in this case, it was necessary to delimit precisely what was intended by 'original source'; that is, what was to be considered as the 'purest' kind of Arabic. The actual answer reflects a compromise between the old tribal idea that the best kind of Arabic was that which was spoken by the camel-herding tribes originating from Central Arabia, and the new Islamic scale of values in which the sedentary Mekkan tribe of Qurayš, in which the Prophet of Islam had been born, came to play a central part; especially since the Qur'ān reflected, in some points, the specific linguistic usage of Mekka. Moreover, it was agreed that these tribes had only kept their purity of language for a limited period: from about the middle of the second/eighth century onwards too frequent contact with non-Arabs had brought about a gradual but irreversible decay of their linguistic usage, so that it could no longer be accepted as authoritative.

Within these limits, any form, word, construction, or utterance used or produced by at least one 'reference speaker' or accepted by him or her as correct ought to be accepted as authentic and to be accounted for within the grammatical system. Even if it exhibited a flagrant deviation from the most current and accepted kind of facts, it could not be rejected as 'incorrect', as the axiom of the system was that the Arabs, and only they, were exempt from barbarism (*laḥn*). The corpus of data gathered in this way comprised first and foremost the Qur'ān, all the canonical recensions of which were considered as authoritative within linguistic studies (as they were in religious sciences); then the old tribal poetry, generally in the form of isolated lines; the *šawāhid* ('witnesses'); together with well-known Beduin proverbs and sayings (*maṯal sā'ir*). On the other hand, *ḥadīṯ* (i.e. the reports about the words and deeds of the Prophet, which are one of the main sources of Islamic law) was pronounced unreliable as linguistic data; the reason invoked is that *ḥadīṯ* transmitters were often of non-Arabic origin, and tended to report only the general meaning of what the Prophet had actually said, while changing the words he had pronounced.

This last point brings us to the second set of criteria, that relating to the transmission of data; a most important issue, since the bulk of the grammatical corpus (including the Qur'ān itself) had originally been transmitted through mainly oral channels. It was quite generally accepted, moreover, that knowledge ought to be transmitted by word of mouth through direct contact between teacher and pupil, and not through written sources usually full of copyists' errors and misreadings. A piece of data, accordingly, could only be accepted if it was transmitted by scholars of recognized status, which vouched for its authenticity. For practical purposes, actually, this principle went quite far; for instance, an anonymous line of verse, which ought theoretically to have been rejected as unreliable since it was impossible to know if it had been composed by an authorized speaker, could still be accepted if some early grammarian or philologist had passed it as authentic.

Such, then, are the 'primary' data on which the Arabic linguistic tradition elaborated its several areas of knowledge; but they are not, by a far cry, the only ones, or even the most numerous. If we examine any grammatical treatise, we soon find that, in the overwhelming majority of cases, grammarians prefer to discuss or illustrate the rules and principles they lay down by way of examples expressly made for the purpose, such as the ubiquitous *ḍaraba Zaydun ʿAmran* ('Zayd hit ʿAmr'), and that they mostly have recourse to real corpus data in order to document some little-known or disputed facts. This way of proceeding is legitimated by the *uṣūl al-naḥw* authors on the grounds that there is no need to authenticate facts which are generally agreed upon as a matter of common knowledge among specialists, such as the fact that the subject of a verbal sentence is in the nominative and its object in the accusative; or, to put it another way, documentation of such commonplace facts would be possible, but pointless.

In other cases, however, such secondary data created and used by grammarians can have a purely technical status within the theory. Such, for instance, is the case of hypothetical utterances created in order to discuss the validity of a rule or principle which cannot be documented in a transparent way by primary data. Data of this kind can be either labelled as unacceptable (the argument running something like: 'If such and such a rule obtained, it would follow that the Arabs would say such and such a thing, which they do not, as they say something else instead'); or it can be considered acceptable, on the grounds that the rule is well founded on other attested facts, and that it is not established that the Arabs did *not* say it; or it can be controverted, some grammarians accepting it and some others rejecting it. To this same category belong data which, however unattestable, must be postulated at an abstract level in order to account for actual constructions (*taqdīr*, see Chap. 3). One could also mention the 'exercise questions' (*masā'il al-tamrīn*), devised to test the learner's abstract mastery of the rules by making him or her apply them to quite improbable utterances.

The second category of problems, collectively referred to as *axḏ al-luġa* ('acceptance of the data') arose from the necessity of bringing some sort of order within this wide and, up to a point, heterogeneous corpus of data. Grammarians, as we have already said, had a strong sense that linguistic facts, for all their apparent disorder, were regulated by an underlying system which it was their task to make visible, in the form of explicit rules and principles. These rules and principles, moreover, were expected, even if only for teaching purposes, to reflect primarily what was considered as most representative of *kalām al-ʿArab*, leaving in the background such marginal data as tribal dialectalisms, archaic words and phrases, or rare constructions and forms of the kind that could be found, for instance, in some pieces of verse when the poet had to depart from the most current way of speaking in order to keep with the necessities of metre and rhyme (these were technically known as *ḍarā'ir al-šiʿr*, 'poetical constraints'). But, on the other hand, grammarians could not completely ignore these 'marginal' data, as they were an integral part of *kalām al-ʿArab*, and, consequently, had to be found a place within the general system of the language. Moreover, even the most current kind of facts exhibited many irregularities and exceptions, which had to be accounted for.

Accordingly, a basic distinction was made between 'regular' (*muṭṭarid*) and 'irregular' (*šāḏḏ*) facts, and a methodological principle laid down, that no valid generalization could be founded on irregular facts (*al-šāḏḏ lā yuqāsu ʿalay-hi*). This actually meant two things: first, that the learner had only to memorize such facts individually, but could not use them to produce any new utterance; and second, that they could not be accepted as valid counterexamples to more general rules relying upon well-attested regularities. But this did not mean that 'irregular' facts were considered by grammarians as mere arbitrary idiosyncrasies which ought to be accepted as such without any attempt at explaining them: such an attitude would have contradicted the postulate that *kalām al-ʿArab* was wholly ordered and systematic. Accordingly, grammarians devoted considerable energy and ingenuity to show that these facts did fall within the general system of the language, even if it was necessary, in order to explain their peculiar behaviour, to allow the most common rules and principles to apply somewhat idiosyncratically, that is out of their usual context, or, conversely, to block their application when it would have produced some unwanted form. But then, these departures from the most common rules and principles was not considered as arbitrary; on the contrary, the grammarians felt that they could, and had to, be explained in terms of general principles, or, as we would say nowadays, of global constraints. Two of these principles play a major part, notably, in morphophonology: the 'heaviness' constraint (*istiṯqāl*), which in substance predicts that some sequences of glides and vowels should be avoided; and the 'non-ambiguity' constraint (*manʿ al-iltibās*), which predicts that crucial morphological information must be recuperable through the 'surface' form (see Chap. 4). The interplay of these two principles was theoretically supposed to account for every case, however irregular it appeared at first glance. For instance, the 'aberrant' plural of *qaws* ('bow'), *qisiyy*, was derived from an underlying form *quwuws*, which exhibits the normal plural pattern for the CaCC nouns (cf. *qalb/quluwb*), first by metathesis (*naql*), giving an intermediate form, *qusuww*, then by the normal application of the *w*-to-*y* 'mutation' (*qalb*) rule when the *w* occurs at the end of a word of more than three non-syllabic elements. So, the only 'idiosyncratic' process here is the metathesis; but then, it is justified in terms of heaviness, as the underlying form exhibits an 'ugly' (*mustakrah*) *uwuw* sequence, which the metathesis helps to eliminate by 'feeding' it to the *w*-to-*y* rule, that is by displacing it in such a context that it will be regularly 'mutated' into a 'lighter' *iyy* sequence (see al-Mubarrad, *Muqtaḍab*, I: 39–41).

Seeming anomalies could also be accounted for in terms of differences between ancient tribal dialects, notably when there existed two alternative forms for the same word, or two different constructions for the same verb or particle. The most remarkable use of this kind of explanation is what is technically called 'commingling of dialectal forms' (*tadāxul al-luḡāt*), which plays an important part in morphology. A most common instance of how this principle works is given by the discussion on the status of verbs like *ḥasiba/yaḥsibu* ('to regard') which form an exception to the general ablaut rule, as the regular imperfect of the verbs of the *fa'ila* class is *yaf'alu*, not *yaf'ilu*, which normally corresponds to a *fa'ala* perfect (see below, p. 79). The classical explanation of this fact is that, originally, there existed two alternative, but equally regular, forms for this verb, as some speakers said *ḥasiba/yaḥsabu*, and some others *ḥasaba/yaḥsibu* (incidentally, both verbs are attested in Standard Classical Arabic, but with somewhat different meanings); then a third group of speakers created a third, hybrid form, by combining the perfect of the first, *ḥasiba*, with the imperfect of the second, *yaḥsibu*. But verbs of this kind (there are a few others) must not be considered in any way as forming a class in themselves, nor as really exceptional to the ablaut rule, as they are only the result of a natural evolution within the general system of the language.

Linguistic facts, then, could be approached at two distinct levels, each corresponding to different practices. At the first level, grammarians had to teach the correct linguistic use, under the form of general rules and principles based upon the most current and representative data, so that they could safely be used in order to generate new forms and utterances. At this level exceptional or 'deviant' data had only to be memorized by the learner in order for him or her to recognize and use them whenever necessary. But, at the second level it was necessary to show that these exceptional data were not arbitrary, and that they could be found a place within the general system of the language, or, in other terms, that they were the product of the most normal and common rules and processes applied in unusual circumstances.

The integrative logic of *qiyās*

One of the basic notions that underly the epistemological conceptions of the Arab grammarians (and possibly of all Islamic scholars) is that identifying an entity's status (its *ḥukm*, that is, literally, the judgement it is liable to) is the key to explaining its nature and properties. Now, the *ḥukm* is something which an entity gets from the place it occupies in the general order of things and which it shares, to some extent, with all entities having an identical or similar position in the relevant system of classification of beings. In many cases recognizing this position and hence identifying the entity's *ḥukm* is rather straightforward and only entails common sense and a basic acquaintance with the proper classificatory system which suits the phenomena under study.

In other instances, however, this recognition is by no means obvious and one may be at a loss to identify where the entity investigated fits in the general order of things and consequently what its normal behaviour may be expected to be. It is in such cases that the process of reasoning known as *qiyās* (literally 'measuring', 'evaluating') is called for.

The usual rendering of the term *qiyās* as 'deduction by analogy' is rather infelicitous, if not altogether misleading, for a number of reasons. The main one is that in many (possibly most) instances of *qiyās* the process of reasoning involved is by no means deductive but rather inductive, the problem being to recognize a particular and usually quite singular entity as an instance of a general type notwithstanding the peculiarities which it presents and which might obscure the fact that it indeed belongs to an already existing and well-known class of phenomena. Moreover, even if the process of reasoning put to use in some instances of *qiyās* proceeds from the general to the particular, it does not seem proper to describe it as a mere deduction, for it generally lacks the deterministic and procedural aspects which make pure deductions both automatic and compelling.

What seems characteristic of *qiyās* in all its forms is its heuristic character: building a *qiyās* consists in exploring an unknown configuration of data and trying to recognize in it a patterning already met and which, in other situations, lent itself to analysis. If such a patterning emerges, then *qiyās* may proceed by assigning to the data of the new configuration a status similar to that of those entities in the reference situation which most closely pattern in an analogous way. The *qiyās* is recognized as valid if this status assignment does indeed lead to a better perception of the configuration of data under investigation.

If this sketchy characterization of *qiyās* is not grossly mistaken, then this process of reasoning should best be viewed as a kind of gestaltist approach that seeks to recognize the pregnant form in any set of objects and to assign to each element of that set a status reflecting that identification. This entails at least three conclusions.

First, this way of understanding *qiyās* explains why two different experts may very well be at variance on the validity of a given *qiyās* bearing on the very same set of data: identifying a form as pregnant is by no means a necessary and univocal process, as opposed to reaching a deductive conclusion after the premises are set. In other words, the results of a *qiyās* may always be questioned, either because the initial global identification of the new situation to an older one is contested, or because the specific conclusions drawn from that basic recognition may not be shared by everyone. On the other hand, the domain of application of *qiyās* is immensely wider than that of any sort of syllogistic reasoning, being only conditioned by the ability of the practitioner to identify a new situation as basically similar to an older one.

Second, it should not be surprising, on these grounds, to observe that the same set of data may lend itself to multiple and very different instances of *qiyās*, depending on the kind of relations one wishes to highlight in that set of data and the background against which these relations are highlighted. As a real example of this situation, consider the case of the passive participle of primitive verbs with second radical [w]: the sweeping majority of them exhibits a [maCūC] pattern which is irregular with respect to the general pattern of such forms for the 'normal' primitive verb, that is [maCCūC]. Now, there exist a few verbs of this class which exhibit the standard [maCCūC] pattern for their passive participle. Al-Mubarrad is said to have considered them as 'regular' (*qiyāsī*) forms on the basis of their likeness to the passive participle of the normal verb. Sībawayhī, on the other hand, considered that the local normal patterning for such forms is the 'abnormal' structure exhibited by the majority of verbs belonging to that special category and that, consequently, the few verbs which functioned in a different way had to be treated as irregular. One of the consequences, of course, was that one could not, on the basis of Sībawayhī's *qiyās*, generate new forms of passive participle with second radical [w] on the pattern of those of the regular verb.

Third, this characterization of *qiyās* also makes it possible to understand why both induction and deduction may be involved in it: *qiyās* is the initial heuristic process by which new data are intuitively grasped as potentially presenting relations known to hold in an already met organization of things. As such, it is independent of the kind of exploitation to which this intuition might lead.

A rather good example of when and how *qiyās* is resorted to in the study of grammatical questions is to be found in a chapter of al-Zağğāğī's *Īḍāḥ* (pp. 64–6) devoted to the assessment of 'explanations in grammar' (*'ilal al-naḥw*). According to that author there are three levels of explanation in linguistic matters. The first one, which he terms 'didactic' (*'illa ta'līmiyya*), merely consists of general statements of facts: e.g. that the subject of a verbal sentence bears the mark of the nominative, that the active participle is normally built after the pattern *fā'il*, or that the assertive particle *inna* assigns the accusative to the theme and the nominative to the predicate in a nominal sentence. This kind of 'explanation' represents all the learner has to know in order to master the correct linguistic usage. It is at the next level that *qiyās* comes into play, and then specifically concerning *inna*. The reason for this is that this word's syntactical behaviour, namely its ability to assign case markers to two following nouns, is rather unusual for the class of particles (which are normally expected either not to determine case assignment at all or to determine it only on the immediately following word). The *qiyās* explanation (*'illa qiyāsiyya*) will precisely consist in reducing this strange behaviour to something more familiar, and presenting an analogous configuration. The central point of this explanation will be to recognize that with its assigning the accusative to a noun and the nominative to another, *inna* configures linguistic data as would a transitive verb whose object would have been anteposed to its subject, as in *ḍaraba axā-ka Muḥammadun* ('he hit your-brother-acc. Muhammad-nom.', i.e. 'it's your brother Muhammad hit'). This recognition may constitute the basis of an explanation of *inna*'s (and its 'sisters' ') behaviour if one is ready to admit that this type of particle somehow 'resembles' (*ḍāra'at*) the transitive verb and hence has been treated (by the speakers of the language) like it with regard to case assignment. As far as this case is concerned, the *qiyās* explanation ends with the admission that the configuration of *inna* and its arguments is formally similar to that of a transitive verb with its specifiers. Then discussion may be pursued at the third level, that of the 'dialectic explanation' (*'illa ğadaliyya*), which will propose diverse justifications for the now admitted resemblance between *inna* and transitive verbs.

This example is significant in that it clearly shows that the basic function of *qiyās* in the general economy of Islamic scholarship is essentially to ensure the integration of new or unfamiliar situations within the framework of already manageable facts. One of the traditional definitions of *qiyās* points to this basic function in a both insightful and misleading way. It says that *qiyās* is the process by which a 'derived' (*farʿ*) entity is related to the 'basic' (*aṣl*) entity to which it belongs on the basis of the recognition of a common element between the two. This definition both reveals the crucial 'integrative' function of *qiyās* and hides its essentially heuristic and so to say 'tentative' aspect: you can say that an entity is 'derived' only after the *qiyās* has successfully led to the identification of its 'basic' gestalt. But this is a consequence of *qiyās*, not a definition of it.

A secondary development of *qiyās*, in the specific field of linguistic studies, has been to function as a generator of new linguistic forms. The basic idea underlying this mechanism is that once an analogy has been recognized between two forms, and in the case when the first one is known to be derivationally related to a series of subforms, then it is considered lawful to generate for the second form the same series of subforms, even though these forms have never been attested in linguistic usage. In this sense, *qiyās* has come to be considered as the antonym of *samāʿ*, the pure reporting of linguistic usage as it has been transmitted from the ancient Arabs. The previous example on passive-participle formation is a typical case, explaining the passage from the general to this secondary acceptation of *qiyās*.

Grammar and reality

A question which must be raised here is whether the explanations the grammarian proposes for the facts he studies correspond, for the Arabic linguistic tradition, to some kind of reality in the mind of the speakers of the language (we of course mean those Beduin Arabs whose profile was sketched in the previous section).

The first to have proposed an answer to this question, here again following a tradition transmitted by al-Zağğāğī (*Īḍāḥ*: 65–6) is al-Xalīl.

> He was asked, concerning the linguistic explanations he endeavoured to set forth: 'Do you hold them from the Arabs or did you invent them yourself?'. He answered: 'The Arabs

> spoke by instinct and natural disposition. They knew the places appropriate for their speech, and the reasons for their linguistic behavior lay in their minds even though they have not been transmitted to us. As for me, I try to find the right explanation in my analyses and if I succeed then so much the better! Although I do know that another one might exist.

The search for the reasons (*ʿilal*) present in the mind of the Arabs and which would account for their linguistic behaviour will reach its apex in the fourth/tenth century in Ibn Ǧinnī's *Xaṣā'iṣ*. On page after page, its author takes great pains to define and justify grammatical method, and to make its procedures explicit either by direct study or by referring it to the methods used in other Islamic sciences. He writes:

> You have to know that the explanations (*ʿilal*) of the grammarians resemble more those of the theologians (*mutakallimūn*) than those of the jurists (*mutafaqqihūn*). This is due to the fact that the grammarians, contrary to the jurists, refer to immediate perception (*ḥiss*) and base themselves on the impression of heaviness or lightness which may be felt in a given situation.
>
> (*Xaṣā'iṣ*, I: 48)

One should not be mistaken, however: the impression of heaviness or lightness (which will be discussed in more detail later; see p. 80) is neither that of the grammarian nor that of his contemporaries, but that of the ancient Arabs or, for lack of them, of the living Beduins likely to have retained their ancestors' linguistic feeling.

Ibn Ǧinnī considered that there existed a basic affinity between these speakers' natural wisdom (*ḥikma*) and the harmonious perfection of the language they spoke. This made it possible for them to grasp spontaneously the natural balance existing in the language and to modulate consciously their linguistic behaviour in accordance with it, in particular by resorting to such expedients as avoiding sequences likely to alter that balance. A special chapter of the *Xaṣā'iṣ* is specifically devoted to showing that Arabs did have a clear perception of the finalized behaviour which grammarians attribute to them, and that they manifested, even without any grammatical terminology, a capacity for linguistic analysis quite comparable with that of Ibn Ǧinnī's fellow grammarians. Two examples will illustrate this.

The first one (Ibn Ǧinnī, *Xaṣā'iṣ*, I: 249) has to do with the object of the participle, which may be either accusative or genitive. For the Arab grammarians, however, the basic case is the accusative construction with the participle bearing 'nūnation' (i.e. adding the [n] suffix to the case ending), while the genitive one, without nūnation on the participle, is the derived case only justified by the search for lightness. The linguistic form under discussion was verse 40 of sura XXXVI (*Yāsīn*) and more specifically the passage saying 'neither night preceding day. . .'.

> Abū ʿAlī [al-Fārisī, Ibn Ǧinnī's master], told us an anecdote reported by Abū Bakr who held it from Abū l-ʿAbbās [the Prophet's uncle]: I once heard 'Umāra B. ʿAqīl . . . reading: "*wa-lā l-laylu sābiqu l-nahāri*" [i.e. the genitive construction] so I asked him what he meant by that and he answered: "*sābiqun al-nahāra*" [with the accusative construction]; – And why didn't you say it in this way? – If I had it would have been more ponderous.

Ibn Ǧinnī goes on to say:

> Three conclusions may be drawn from this story: first a confirmation of our analysis which says that the basic case is the accusative; then another confirmation of our analysis which says that the reason for the change from the basic case to the derived one aims at lightness: it is obvious that this Beduin was indeed seeking lightness, as is shown by his commentary: 'this would have been more ponderous', that is 'heavier on the mind and stronger', as when they say: 'this dirham is more ponderous', that is 'heavy'. The third conclusion is that the Arabs were likely to use a term while having another, stronger one, in mind just for the sake of lightness.

The second example (Ibn Ǧinnī, *Xaṣā'iṣ*, I: 250) has to do with the use of case markers: nominative for the subject and accusative for the direct object.

> One day I asked al-Šaǧarī: "Hey Abū ʿAbdallāh, how do you say "I hit your brother [accusative]"? – Just that way. – Would you then say "I hit your brother [nominative]"? – No, I never say "your brother [nominative]"! I said: – How

then do you say "your brother [nominative] hit me" – Just that way, he said. – Haven't you just pretended, I said, that you never say "your brother [nominative]"? – What's that, he said! the aspects of the speech are different!' Does this mean something different from us saying the object has become subject? Even though it is not with the same words it is undoubtedly the same thing.

In short, in Ibn Ǧinnī's opinion speakers are grammarians without knowing it, and capable, thanks to their inherent wisdom, of making the very generalizations which the professionals of grammar try to formulate.

The idea that there is an affinity between the wisdom of speakers and the design of the language is probably not specific to the traditional Arabic approach. It should be stressed, however, that in the case at hand it was set in the specific ideological context of the new Islamic society (for more details of this context see Chap. 5) and hence this idea was limited to the Arabic language, the only one recognized as constituting a coherent whole.

> This precluded, consequently, any problematics of language considered as the set of properties common to all tongues. Not that grammarians systematically reject the existence of such properties, but simply they do not consider them as interesting. In other words, the Arabic grammatical tradition never evolved towards the direction of a general grammar.
> (J.-P. Guillaume, 1986: 140f.)

This also had the effect of 'blocking grammatical analysis in a strictly synchronic perspective: facts have to be described and explained within the system as it is given in the sole state of language available' (ibid.).

This bias towards the exclusive recognition of Arabic as a perfectly harmonious system may very well be the ultimate explanation of Ibn Ǧinnī's ambivalent attitude on the question of the origin of language. On the one hand, he seems to appreciate the thesis of a natural genesis of languages, all languages, from the imitation of sounds heard by humans in their natural environment. He writes, concerning this:

> Some think that the origin of all languages is in the sound that one can hear such as that of the wind, that of the thunder, the murmur of waters, the braying of donkeys, the

> cawing of ravens, the neighing of horses, the troating of stags. Then languages developed from that. This is a sound opinion and an acceptable view.
>
> (*Xaṣā'iṣ*, I: 46f.)

But then, and, as it seems, concerning the specific case of Arabic, he adds: 'The more I reflect on that venerable, noble and subtle language, the more I find in it manifestations of wisdom, of precision and finesse. . .' (ibid.). And all this strengthens in his mind the view that this language could well be of divine inspiration. He does not, as a matter of fact, discard the idea that God could have created, in the past, people with a subtler intelligence than ours who would consequently have been able, by convention, to institute the Arabic language. But the important thing is the perplexity he feels about all that: 'I stand between these two possibilities, exhausted and overwhelmed, incapable of choosing between one and the other' (*Xaṣā'iṣ* ,I: 47).

2

SĪBAWAYHI'S *KITĀB*: AN ENUNCIATIVE APPROACH TO SYNTAX

For quite a long time it was generally agreed by both western and eastern Arabists that Sībawayhi's *Kitāb* contained, even be it in an incipient and somewhat unsystematic and disordered way, what was to become the classical formulation of grammatical theory. Of course, it was admitted that some differences existed on some points between Sībawayhi's views and those of such and such later grammarian, but then they were usually explained away as merely terminological, or as ordinary instances of the fact that some degree of disagreement on minor issues was commonly accepted as legitimate within the Arabic tradition. True to say, this view of Sībawayhi's place within the development of AGT, embodied in its most representative form in Jahn's translation of the *Kitāb* (Jahn, 1895–1900), was based on the explicit statements of the grammarians themselves. These never ceased to refer to Sībawayhi as the main founding father of their discipline, quoting his views and commenting his analyses as if no difference existed between his approach and their own.

Moreover, the fact that most Arabists approached grammatical texts from a philological point of view led them to concentrate upon 'facts', that is the linguistic data gathered within grammatical treatises, at the expense of more theoretical aspects. From this point of view at least, Fleisch's (1969: 46) claim that 'les grammairiens reprennent . . . (fastidieusement) les mêmes exemples que Sībawayhi' ('grammarians (tediously) repeat the same examples as Sībawayhi') seems reasonable, if perhaps not very perceptive of what is really important in AGT. Finally, a third factor made it difficult, indeed nearly impossible, to grasp fully the historical evolution of AGT: the lack of available published sources. For a very long time (in fact down to the

1950s), the only available grammatical treatises in Arabic, apart from the *Kitāb* itself, were late Classical works used as teaching manuals in Islamic universities. It is quite symptomatic that the only fourth/tenth-century grammarian quoted first-hand in such a comparatively recent and deeply erudite work as Fleisch (1961: xvi–xvii and 19–49 *passim*) is Ibn Ǧinnī, whose main works had been published only a few years before, between 1952 and 1960 (ibid.: 36).

All these factors explain why it was only in the late 1960s that Carter (1968) first advanced the thesis, which, reasoning *ex post facto*, seems quite obvious, that the traditional interpretation of the *Kitāb* was a classical instance of *husteron proteron*, as it relied on the explanations and commentaries found in later treatises (peculiarly, in the case of Jahn, the *Šarḥ al-Mufaṣṣal*). Carter further claimed that, if one made abstraction of these commentaries and went back to the original text, the picture which emerged of Sībawayhi's system was massively different from that of the later grammarians, which had come to be assimilated from the time of Silvestre de Sacy (1831) with the whole Arabic tradition.

At another level, and some years later, this will to go back to the original text also appears in Troupeau's work on Sībawayhi's terminology (Troupeau, 1976). The French equivalents he gives attempt to reflect the fact that, at the period in which the *Kitāb* was written, the specific metalanguage of grammar was not yet fully autonomous from ordinary usage; so that many grammatical terms which in later periods came to be considered merely conventional (and hence feebly motivated, or not at all) were originally metaphors (in which the intended meaning is only recuperable by reference to the ordinary, lexical sense of the term), these metaphors being in many cases possibly forged by Sībawayhi himself. At approximately the same time the publication of Ibn al-Sarrāǧ's *Kitāb al-Uṣūl*, first in Iraq in 1973 then in Lebanon in 1985, made possible a global re-evaluation of the history of ALT and of Sībawayhi's place within it, as we tried to show in Chapter 1.

It should be stressed, however, that many Arabists do not accept the notion that the *Kitāb* reflects in any relevant way a basically different conception of grammatical analysis from the classical grammarians'. Moreover, if our own interpretation certainly owes a lot to Carter's and Troupeau's works, it is yet substantially different from the conclusions of either. Actually, readers will have grasped that the problem we treat here is one of the less consensual in the discipline, the more so as it is crucially related to this major bone of contention, the question of the origins of the Arabic grammatical tradition.

PROBLEMS AND HYPOTHESES

Interpreting the *Kitāb*

The main difficulty in discussing Sībawayhi's approach is that, contrary to what is the case with classical grammarians, he never explicitly states the basic theoretical principles on which he works. Admittedly, the first seven chapters of the *Kitāb*, traditionally known as its *Risāla* ('Preliminary epistle'), expound some preliminary notions such as the parts of speech, or the system of mood and case markers (*iʿrāb*) and so forth; but these questions are treated, for the main part, quite independently from each other, and indeed appear so loosely connected that it is impossible to derive from them any clear idea about the object and methods of grammar according to Sībawayhi. Actually, the most plausible hypothesis is that these chapters were never intended for such a purpose, and that their aim was only to provide the reader with some general information about several basic descriptive concepts and devices of grammar, and not to state formally what grammar is.

As for the bulk of the work, it seems at first sight no less baffling; it apparently consists of a set of more or less independent chapters, each one being devoted to a particular question. The connection between successive chapters can vary considerably; in some cases there is hardly a connection at all, while in others the subject-matter of two or more chapters seems to overlap in a complex manner, and, in others still, connection is explicitly or implicitly made between chapters widely distant from each other. In spite of all this, however, the book gives a subtle impression of conscious ordering and progression, even if this ordering is not based upon a rigidly hierarchical system of categories, as is the case with classical treatises, but on a more delicate balance between the reader's intuitive knowledge about linguistic facts and the necessity to bring him or her to a deeper and more self-conscious apprehension of the underlying generalities which govern these facts.

The same reliance on the reader's intuition appears in the organization of each individual chapter. Typically, Sībawayhi's method consists in giving all the relevant data, together with some generally quite informal remarks about their degree of acceptability or their relation to each other. Whenever syntax is concerned, this approach substantially amounts to constructing a class of related utterances, and then to show, usually by way of paraphrase, the differences between them.

As an illustration of this aspect of Sībawayhi's method, we shall briefly analyse here the thirtieth chapter of the *Kitāb*, devoted to 'the verbs which can be made to govern or prevented from it' (*Bāb al-afʿāl allatī tustaʿmal wa-tulġā*, I: 61–4). This rather cryptic formulation refers to a peculiarity of the 'cognitive verbs' (*afʿāl al-qulūb*), such as *ʿalima* ('to know') or *ẓanna* ('to suppose'), which are normally constructed with a double accusative, e.g. *aẓunnu Zaydan ḏāhiban* ('I suppose Zayd-acc. going-away-acc.'), but can in some cases occur with a double nominative, e.g. *Zaydun ḏahibun aẓunnu* ('Zayd-nom. is going-away-nom. I suppose'). These two constructions are respectively called *iʿmāl* or (especially in the *Kitāb*) *istiʿmāl*, that is 'making use of [the verb's capacity to] govern', and *ilġa'*, that is 'abolishing [the verb's capacity to govern]'. In the first case, the assignation of the accusative to *Zayd* and *ḏāhib* is considered to be effected by the verb's government, while, in the second, this government is 'suspended', so that the other two elements are marked by the nominative, according to the processes of case assignation within the nominal sentence.

After having listed the six verbs which are affected by this construction, Sībawayhi proceeds to review the different possible utterances which can be formed on this basis, beginning by the most 'normal', i.e. unmarked, case, that of *istiʿmāl*. In the following list we have 'normalized' his examples for clarity's sake.

(1) With *istiʿmāl*:
  (a) Aẓunnu Zaydan ḏāhiban
  'I believe Z. going away.'
  (b) Zaydan aẓunnu ḏāhiban
  'It is Z. I believe going away.'
  (c) Zaydun aẓunnu-hu ḏāhiban
  'Z., I believe him going away.'
  (d) Zaydan aẓunnu-hu ḏāhiban
  'It is Z. I believe him going away.' (*sic*)

(e) Aẓunnu Zaydan munṭaliqan wa-ʿAmran aẓunnu-hu xāriǧan
'I believe Z. going away, and ʿAmr I believe him going out.'

(f) Zaydan munṭaliqan aẓunnu
'Z. going away, I believe.'

In this paradigm, (1a) represents the most normal case, as it respects the canonical word ordering, where the object follows the verb. Examples (1b) and (1c) represent two current cases of anteposition: in the former, the anteposed element keeps its status as object of the verb, as is shown by the fact that it exhibits the accusative; while in the latter, it is analysed as a theme (*mubtadaʾ*) regularly marked with the nominative, while the formal object of the verb is the anaphoric pronoun *-hu*. As for (1d), Sībawayhi stresses that such a pattern is only accepted by some speakers and, while not actually incorrect, is better avoided, unless, as in (1e), it is coordinated with another sentence.

(2) With *ilǧāʾ*:

(a) Zaydun aẓunnu d̲āhibun
'Z., I believe, has gone away.'

(b) Zaydun d̲āhibun aẓunnu
'Z. has gone away, I believe.'

(c) Aẓunnu Zaydun d̲āhibun
'I believe, Z. has gone away.'

It is only after he has listed all these utterances that Sībawayhi embarks on a somewhat more abstract discussion; its point of departure is the difference between examples (2a–c):

> Any time you intend ilǧaʾ, postposition [i.e. of the cognitive verb, as in (2a)] is stronger, although all [these examples] are good Arabic. . . . The reason why postposition is stronger is that he [i.e. the speaker] brings forth the doubt [i.e. the modality expressed by the verb *ẓanna*] after his utterance has been completed on the mode of certainty [as in (2b)], or after it has begun as if it intended to express certainty and was afterwards affected with doubt [as in (2a)]. . . . And if he begins his utterance in a way which expresses that he is in doubt, he makes the verb to govern [as in (1a–f)], whether he anteposes [the object] or not, just like he says *Zaydan raʾaytu* ('[It is] Z-acc. [that] I saw') or *raʾaytu Zaydan* ('I saw

> Z.') [cf. (1a) and (1b), respectively]. The longer the utterance is, the weaker postposition becomes if the verb has government [as in (1f)] . . . , since the general rule is that the verb begins the sentence whenever it has government.
>
> (*Kitāb*, I: 61)

The rest of the chapter is devoted to other questions related to the behaviour of these verbs in some specific cases, which will not detain us here. The important thing is that the above fragment exemplifies, in a most typical fashion, the main difficulties raised by Sībawayhi's approach. Actually, the problem is not to understand, at first degree, his rather straightforward and matter-of-fact remarks, but to discern the theoretical principles which underlie them, or even, at a more modest level, to distinguish in a text such as this between those terms which have a formal theoretical status as grammatical categories and those which do not. Of course, reasoning *a posteriori* on the basis of what we know about the classical theory, we might be tempted to say that terms which denote formal relationships, materialized through distribution of case-marks (such as *i'māl* or *ilḡā'*), or through word ordering (such as *taqdīm* or *ta'xīr*) have full status as theoretical concepts, and that, conversely, such terms as 'certainty' or 'doubt', such expressions which point at the speaker's intentions or attitudes, should be considered as mere informal glosses and paraphrases, aiming at illustrating facts, at making them more easily understandable by the reader, but not at describing or explaining them in a formal sense. But then, of course, we have no reason to assume that Sībawayhi's system is substantially equivalent to the classical grammarians' (indeed, by assuming it we would fall back into the petition of principle pointed out by Carter). Moreover, even if we did, we would only be confronted by new problems, as even a perfunctory glance at the above fragment shows that it is nearly impossible to distinguish between 'formal' statements giving a description of facts and 'informal' ones paraphrasing them.

This rather baffling situation, moreover, appears in nearly every chapter of the *Kitāb*. The facts are usually quite easy to grasp (even if the reason why some particular kinds of facts appear together with some others occasionally needs some time to figure out), the explanations given about them seem, at first glance, quite reasonable and straightforward, but the problem is: what are we to do with them? Unless one is ready to treat the *Kitāb* as a disjointed collection of local analyses with little or no internal coherency (a rather forlorn perspective, at best), it seems necessary to look for a general model, in terms of which it is possible to make global sense of the *Kitāb*. Of course, given the complexity of the problems, many hypotheses are *a priori* possible, depending on the aspect of Sībawayhi's system one considers as fundamental. The method followed by most Arabists for this purpose is to delimit a set of key concepts on the basis of which a global hypothesis is constructed. Carter's interpretation, for instance, is based on the assumption that terms such as *mawḍiʿ* and *manzila* (which he translates by 'function' and 'status', respectively) or *ḥasan* and *qabīḥ* (which denote the well-formedness of an utterance or the lack of it) give the key to Sībawayhi's approach to language. In reconstructing this approach, Carter takes into account not only the technical meaning of these terms within the *Kitāb*, but also the ethical and juridical connotations they imply, in order to show that '[Sībawayhi] chose human society as a metaphor through which to express the linguistic facts' (Carter, 1980: 26).

While there is no denying that Carter's interpretation is both ingenious and far-reaching, and that it contributed in a large degree to renew the field of Sībawayhian studies, we must frankly acknowledge that we cannot accept it wholesale. In particular, we feel that the methodology on which it is based does not seem completely free from arbitrariness: what cause do we have to say, for instance, that *mawḍiʿ* and *manzila* (which are, by the way, commonly used by classical grammarians) are more relevant to Sībawayhi's global approach to language than, say, *binā'* ('[syntactic] construction') or *arāda* ('to intend'), which seem much more frequent within the text of the *Kitāb*? More generally speaking, we are thrown back upon the problem we evoked earlier: how can we distinguish, within the text, between authentic theoretical concepts and mere illustrative paraphrase? But then, one could ask, is it really necessary to distinguish formally between the two? Or, to put it differently, must a hypothesis on Sībawayhi's approach be built merely on the basis of his terminology, or could it be done by addressing oneself to other levels of the text? It is on this last assumption that the hypothesis we will offer here is founded; we readily acknowledge that, in its present form at least, it cannot pretend to account for every single detail in the *Kitāb*, and that on many points it ought to be adjusted and refined. On the other hand, we feel, nevertheless, that it can shed relevant light on many basic aspects of Sībawayhi's approach to grammatical analysis.

The enunciative hypothesis

Typologically, grammatical and linguistic systems can be divided into two rough classes: on the one hand, those which analyse utterances in terms of formal relationships between their components; on the other hand, those which analyse them in terms of operations performed by the speaker in order to achieve a specific effect on the allocutee. Our claim is that Sībawayhi's approach basically belongs to the latter category, while the classical grammarians' typically belongs to the former. Or, to put it more finely, Sībawayhi's system of analysis crucially presupposes that any utterance is the final result of a sequence of operations performed by the speaker, each one of these operations being simultaneously and indissociably formal and semantic.

This will perhaps appear more clearly if we go back to the example cited above, that of *ilġā'* and *iʿmāl*. As we have seen, the first step in Sībawayhi's analysis consists in constructing a family of utterances which correspond more or less to the same global meaning (the speaker says that he believes that Zayd has gone away, although he is not quite sure about it). The first great division within this family is based on the antithetic categories of *iʿmāl* and *ilġā'*. It should be noted here that these terms are *maṣdars* (verbal nouns) derived from factitive verbs, and that they actually point to something performed by the speaker: he can either make the cognitive verb govern (*iʿmāl*) or prevent it from governing (*ilġā'*). Now these two operations, even if they are expressed through terms which denote merely formal properties of the verb (namely, that it assigns such a case marker to such a component of the sentence), are nevertheless related to semantic considerations, that is to the intention (*niyya*) of the speaker. The use of *iʿmāl* suggests that he intends to stress directly that he is not quite sure of what he is about to say, while the use of *ilġā'* suggests that doubt came to him as a kind of afterthought. In other words, *iʿmāl* and *ilġā'* can be considered as two different strategies for saying something one is not sure about; it is up to the speaker to choose whichever is most appropriate to the situation.

But then, in whichever case, new operations have to be performed in order to give the utterance its definitive form. These operations, which relate to word order, are traditionally called *taqdīm wa-ta'xīr* ('anteposition and postposition'). Here again, these terms etymologically refer to operations performed by the speaker, with a specific intention. Although Sībawayhi's analysis of the semantic aspects of such operations is somewhat perfunctory, he stresses that '[the speakers] antepose what they consider most important for them to make clear, and what is most necessary for them to express' (*Kitāb*, I: 15). But the important thing is that all the utterances one can form in this way are not equally felicitous, though in this particular case none can be actually discarded as incorrect. If, at the first level, you choose *iʿmāl*, you had better not antepose both complements as in (1f) ('Zayd-acc. going-away-acc. I think'): since your earlier choice suggested that the doubt you express was, so to speak, built into your utterance, it is somewhat inconsistent to mention it after the thing you are doubtful about. Conversely, if you choose in the first place to express your doubt as an added commentary or an afterthought, you should not normally antepose the verb, as in (2c) ('I believe, Z.-nom. [is] going-away-nom.').

It is now possible, on the basis of this example, to state more precisely and more formally our 'enunciative hypothesis'. First, it should be stressed that Sībawayhi usually does not analyse isolated utterances, but more exactly families of utterances, so as to make apparent both their basic similarity and their individual dissimilarities. Similarities and dissimilarities alike are accounted for in terms of enunciative operations performed at different levels: *iʿmāl* and *ilḡā'*, which have direct consequences on the distribution of case markers, must clearly be performed before *taqdīm* and *ta'xīr*, which operate irrespective of case markers. As a consequence, the degree of similarity and dissimilarity between two related utterances reflects the fact that they have a more or less common 'history'. In our example, utterances (1a–f), which have been constructed through *iʿmāl*, have more in common with each other than they have with utterances (2a–c). Moreover, (1a), (1b), and (1f), which are the product of simple *taqdīm wa-ta'xīr* operations, are nearer to each other than they are to (1c), (1d), and (1e), since each of them supposes the performing of a new operation, such as changing the anteposed complement into a theme in (1c), and so forth.

Each utterance within a given family can, as a consequence, be considered as the result of a specific strategy entailing at every step a choice between different equally possible operations. Each operation, at every stage, is associated with the actualization of a specific semantic value, so that choosing one of them is, in principle, a matter of what the speaker intends to say. However, in some cases, the relative success or failure of a strategy can be assessed irrespective of the speaker's intention; an example of this is given by utterances (1f) and (2c) above (respectively 'Z-acc. gone-away-acc. I believe' and 'I believe Z-nom. is gone-away-nom.'), which, according to Sībawayhi, are 'weak' in any case, that is less successful than the others. The reason why they are so is that they reflect somewhat incoherent choices, in that the semantic value actualized by the operation performed at one level is not fully compatible with the semantic value actualized at another. If you choose *iʿmāl*, you intend to build all your utterance on the modality of doubt; on the other hand, if you antepose an element, you suggest that you consider it, in some way or other, as the most important within the utterance. If you antepose the whole statement that you are doubtful about (represented by the two complements) to the verb which expresses doubt, while giving it a construction suggesting that it is the basic element of the utterance, it becomes impossible to understand precisely whether you intend primarily to express doubt about something, or to state something you are doubtful about. Of course, in this particular case the incompatibility only concerns rather subtle shades of meaning, so that the general intent of the utterance remains recoverable; but one can easily understand that, in other cases, a badly planned strategy can result in a wholly uninterpretable utterance.

This brings us to a quite well-known peculiarity of the *Kitāb*: namely, the richness and complexity of its criteriology. Whereas classical grammarians simply classify utterances on the basis of absolute 'correctness' (*ṣiḥḥa*) or 'incorrectness' (*fasād*), that is conformity to the rules or the lack of it, Sībawayhi uses a subtly and sometimes elusively graduated scale of values in order to express judgements about utterances. The main outlines of this system are put forth in a specific chapter of the *Risāla* (*Kitāb*, I: 8). According to this chapter, utterances can, at a first level, be classified between 'straight' (*mustaqīm*) and 'crooked' (*muḥāl*); the examples show that a 'crooked' utterance is one from which no kind of meaning can be recovered, as, for instance, 'I saw you tomorrow'. At a second level, 'straight' utterances are further divided between 'good' (*ḥasan*) and 'bad' (*qabīḥ*). Once again the examples show that 'bad' sentences are those through which it is possible to recapture some kind of meaning, even if their construction is faulty, such as *qad Zaydan ra'aytu*, which would sound something like 'I John have seen' in English; technically, the construction is faulty because it is impossible to insert something between the pre-verbal particle *qad* and the verb it modifies. But then, if one refers to the bulk of the *Kitāb*, one quickly discovers that those are not the only criteria used by Sībawayhi. We have already seen him qualifying some utterances as 'weak', that is basically correct but somewhat infelicitous. But we also find another set of criteria, relating not to the value of such and such an utterance taken in itself, but to its frequency within the 'speech of the Arabs': an utterance can be declared 'good Arabic' (*ʿArabī ǧayyid*) or 'well-attested Arabic' (*ʿArabī kaṯīr*) and so forth. In some cases there seems to be a compromise between what is actually attested and what the inherent logic of the language makes possible (or impossible). One sometimes gets the impression that what Sībawayhi calls 'weak' utterances are actually 'bad' ones, except that they have been, so to speak, legitimated by the Arabs' attested use of them. In other cases, Sībawayhi explicitly states that, while an utterance such as *qā'iman fī-hā raǧulun* ('Standing up, a man is in it') is theoretically possible, since one can say *rākiban marra raǧulun* ('Riding, a man passed') and since the locative phrase *fī-hā* has the status of a verb, it is impossible to use it, since the Arabs rejected it.

Now we submit that this rather abundant terminology is quite understandable within our hypothesis. If we admit that Sībawayhi considers utterances as the global result of specific strategies, involving, at each level, a choice between several possible solutions, it follows that an adequate criteriology should be able to express the relative degree of success or failure of any given strategy; that is, the extent to which the semantic values actualized by every successive operation performed agree or disagree with each other, or again the extent to which the speaker's intended meaning is recoverable. This offers a wide range of possibilities, from total failure ('crooked' utterances) to complete success ('good' utterances). But such a system, taken in itself, cannot predict exactly which kind of utterances are acceptable and which are not, or, to put it differently, what degree of success an utterance must achieve in order to pass as acceptable. This is where the reference to the 'speech of the Arabs' comes in: the usage of the 'reference speakers' must be accepted as the primary norm in order to distinguish what is 'permissible' (*ǧā'iz*) and what is not.

PREDICATION AND ENUNCIATION: SĪBAWAYHI'S THEORY OF THE UTTERANCE

Since Sībawayhi's whole project could be qualified as an attempt to describe exhaustively all the enunciative operations possible in Arabic, and all the ways they can be combined into different strategies, it would be quite impossible to examine, within the scope of this chapter, all the aspects of his system. We will, therefore, content ourselves with discussing briefly one major aspect of it, which we will call, for simplicity's sake, his 'theory of the utterance'. Properly speaking, however, it is not a theory at all, if by theory we mean a specific set of explicit general statements about something called 'utterance' (or some Arabic equivalent), locatable in a specific portion of the *Kitāb*. Actually, what we will discuss here is an abstract reconstruction on the basis of several chance remarks and disjointed observations passed by Sībawayhi at different places in his work. But what seems most important and significant to us is that these remarks and observations only make sense if one brings them back to a single, coherent set of presuppositions, all the more so as there is nothing in the *Kitāb*, to our knowledge, which explicitly or implicitly goes against these presuppositions.

If our hypothesis is right, we should expect it to have important and significant implications on this aspect of Sībawayhi's system. Broadly speaking, an enunciative approach to the study of utterances would take into account not only the utterance itself, but also its relation to the communicative situation within which it is uttered; or, to use more technical terminology, the relation between the predicative situation (i.e. what is predicated by the utterance) and the enunciative situation. In the following pages, we will try to show that such is actually the case, and that, in several unrelated passages, Sībawayhi crucially and constantly implies that an utterance minimally consists of not two, but three abstract elements, two of them being predicative and the third enunciative.

At first view, such a statement seems to go directly against at least one explicit passage of the *Kitāb*, namely the third chapter of the *Risāla*, entitled *bāb al-musnad wa-l-musnad ilay-hi* (*Kitāb*, I: 7), which one could translate, with some caution, as 'Chapter of the two Components of the Utterance'. Here is the relevant passage:

> They [i.e. the *musnad* and the *musnad ilay-hi*] are what cannot exist independently of each other, and what the speaker cannot dispense with. Among these are the *mubtada'* noun [i.e. the theme of a nominal sentence; see below] and what is built upon it, as when you say *'Abdu-llāh axū-ka* (''A. is your brother') and *hāḏā axū-ka* ('This is your brother'). Like this is *yaḏhabu 'Abdu-llāh* (''A. is going away'): the verb cannot dispense with the noun, just as the first noun [i.e. the *mubtada'* in the above examples] could not dispense with the other in the *ibtidā'* [i.e. the nominal sentence].

Apparently, Sībawayhi means here that an utterance consists minimally in two elements, not more, these elements being either a (nominal) theme and a predicate, or a verb and a noun (which is, in the simplest case, the subject). However, if we read the text more attentively, we realize that this is not exactly what Sībawayhi says. Actually, the only point he explicitly makes is that the *musnad* and the *musnad ilay-hi*, the two predicative elements of an utterance, are strictly interdependent and mutually indispensable, so that no utterance can exist when one of them is lacking. In other words, the presence of two predicative elements is a necessary, not a sufficient, condition. Moreover, it should be stressed that Sībawayhi speaks here of words, not of abstract elements, which are quite different, as we shall see further on.

It seems then that, after all, our problem is not so much with Sībawayhi's text as with its traditional interpretation by classical grammarians, who explicitly stated that a sentence consists minimally of a 'predicand' (*musnad ilay-hi*), being either the theme of a nominal sentence or the subject of a verbal one, and of a 'predicate' (*musnad*), either the predicate (*xabar*) of a nominal sentence, or the verb of a verbal one, these two elements being united by an abstract relationship, *isnād* (see Chapter 3). As very often happens, the classical grammarians, while taking up

Sībawayhi's terminology and formulations, gave it a quite different meaning. This fact, however, did not pass completely unobserved: in the late nineteenth century, F. Praetorius remarked that, apparently, Sībawayhi uses each one of these terms to mean what the classical grammarians mean by the other. For example, in one passage at least, while discussing the utterance *hāḏā Zaydun munṭaliqan* ('Here is Z., going away'), he quite incidentally states that *hāḏā* (i.e. the predicand) is *musnad*, and *Zaydun* (i.e. the predicate) is *musnad ilay-hi* (*Kitāb*, I: 256). For the classical grammarians, it would be exactly the other way round. This observation was in more recent years taken up by Levin (1981) and Goldenberg (1988), who examined some of its implications.

In spite of their considerable erudition and the light they shed on the historical development of the Arabic tradition, these studies suffer, to our minds at least, from the limitations inherent in a merely terminological approach of the *Kitāb*. They tend to assume more or less implicitly that, even if Sībawayhi does not use the terms under discussion exactly in the same way as the classical grammarians do, they nevertheless have the same crucial relevance to his theory of the utterance as they do to, say, al-Zamaxšarī's. Our claim is that such an assumption is both unnecessary and partially misleading: unnecessary because the attestations of the terms *musnad* and *musnad ilay-hi* in the *Kitāb* are so few that one can hardly consider them as central concepts within Sībawayhi's system; misleading, because this assumption results in putting false questions (e.g. wondering what is *musnad* and what *musnad ilay-hi* in a verbal sentence, since Sībawayhi is quite silent on this point) and in not putting good ones.

Actually, if one approaches the text without any preconceived idea about what one should find in it, Sībawayhi's conception of the utterance appears quite simple and straightforward, even if it must be, as always, reconstructed piecemeal from different passages of the *Kitāb*. Expressed in quite simple, ordinary terms (which is perhaps the best way of interpreting Sībawayhi), it runs something like this. Basically there are two modes of speech: either you speak about some person or object already known both by you and your allocutee by giving information (*xabar*) about him, her, or it, this information being supposedly not known by your allocutee; or you speak about a singular event (*ḥadaṯ*) located in time, by specifying the person or object more directly concerned by it (if this event is an action, which is the most usual case, it will normally be the 'doer' or agent, *fā'il*). In the first case, you have a nominal sentence, consisting of a theme and a predicate; in the second a verbal sentence, consisting of a verb and a subject. As it appears from Sībawayhi's most familiar terminology, the semantic aspects of what we call predication are expressed by different terms according to whether it expresses a static property of a given object (nominal sentence) or a dynamic change in the current situation, brought about by a new event (verbal sentence).

The first lines of the 'Chapter of the *Musnad* and *Musnad ilay-hi*' suggests that the main common point between these two structures is that they consist of two elements, and that both of them are equally necessary to the success of any utterance: you cannot speak about something unless you say something about it, and you cannot give information without giving it about something; conversely, you cannot mention an event without specifying what or whom is directly concerned with it. As for the rest of the chapter, it is exclusively devoted to nominal predication. This passage is certainly most important for understanding Sībawayhi's conception of the utterance, and the crucial relationship it establishes between predication and enunciation.

As usual, the passage consists mainly in constructing a family of utterances, which we will begin by listing, for the sake of convenience:

(3) Zaydun munṭaliqun
'Z-nom. [is] departing-nom.'
(4) kāna Zaydun munṭaliqan
'Z-nom. was departing-acc.'
(5) layta Zaydan munṭaliqun
'Would God Z-acc. [was] departing-nom.'
(6) ra'aytu Zaydan munṭaliqan
'I think Z-acc. [is] departing-acc.'
(7) marartu bi-Zaydin munṭaliqan
'I passed by Zayd-gen. departing-acc.'

Sībawayhi, moreover, suggests two important ideas; first, that the interdependence between *Zayd* and *munṭaliq* remains the same in all these examples, irrespective of their syntactic status (indicated by the different case markers they bear); second, that example (3) must be considered as 'primary' (*awwal*) relative to the others, 'just as unity is the first number, and that the indefinite noun is prior to (*qabl*) the definite one'.

Now, if we examine this paradigm, we observe that all the elements which appear in examples (4–7) have two indissociable functions: on the formal level they modify the distribution of case markers; and on the semantic level they modify the way in which the predicative relationship is asserted. It is necessary, then, in order to follow Sībawayhi's train of thought, to distinguish clearly, in all these examples, between an unasserted predicative relationship, which consists of *Zayd* and *munṭaliq*, and a third element whose function it is to express the relation between the current enunciative situation and the predicative situation (i.e. the situation evoked by the predicative relationship, in this case Zayd's being departing). In other words, these elements are equivalent to what some modern enunciative theories (notably A. Culioli's) call 'locators' or 'pointers' (*repères*) (see Culioli 1982).

This leaves us with the first and most basic case, that of example (3): this is usually referred to by Sībawayhi as *ibtidā'*, literally 'the act of beginning'. Actually, this term, in its most original meaning, denotes an operation performed by the speaker; in this respect, it is not very different from the operations which consist in 'inserting' (*idxāl*) any other locator such as *kāna*, *layta*, and so on, the only difference being that it leaves no trace in the actual form of the utterance, except the fact that it assigns the nominative to its two components. But then, it is not to be wondered at, since 'simple' nominal sentences such as (3) precisely suppose that the predicative situation is immediately related to the enunciative situation; in other words, *ibtidā'* can be considered as an operation by which the speaker establishes the enunciative situation itself as locator of the predicative situation.

On these bases, then, it is possible to say that Sībawayhi's conception of the utterance crucially supposes not a twofold but a threefold system, composed of an unasserted binary predicative relationship and of an enunciative locator. But we still have to show how this model applies to the verbal sentence. Apparently it is more difficult, as Sībawayhi never refers to the existence of a necessary third element such as *ibtidā'* when verbal predication is involved. But actually, if we refer to his conception of the verb, it clearly appears that for him it is not a simple unit, but a complex one. This idea is first set out in his well-known definition of the verb:

> [a set of] morphological patterns taken from the pronunciation of the accidents of the nouns [or 'what is reported about the nouns'] and constructed in order to signify what is past, what will be and has not yet happened, and what is currently being and has not ceased to be.
>
> (*Kitāb*, I: 2)

This rather cryptic definition is made somewhat more explicit by a remark some pages later:

> So the nouns [i.e. subjects and assimilated] are that about which something is reported [*muḥaddaṯ ʿan-hā*], and the morphological patterns [i.e. of the verb] signify what is past and what is not past relative to what is reported about the nouns, that is the fact-of-going-away [*ḏahāb*], the fact-of-sitting-down [*ǧulūs*], the fact-of-hitting [*ḍarb*]. The morphological patterns are different from the things reported and the things about which they are reported, that is the nouns.
>
> (*Kitāb*, I: 14)

In other words, Sībawayhi sees the verb as a complex unit, integrating a process (corresponding to a 'verbal noun' (*maṣdar)*, such as *ḏahāb* and the like) within a morphological pattern whose function is to locate the process with reference to the enunciative situation. As the first fragment clearly shows, he considers that the most intrinsically verbal part of the verb, so to speak, is its abstract morphological pattern, while its material part, denoting the generic process involved, is not primarily verbal, since its simplest form is verbal. In such conditions, it is quite clear that, as the second fragment explicitly suggests, a verbal sentence actually consists of three (abstract) elements: 'that about which something is reported' (i.e. the predicand), 'that which is reported' (i.e. the predicate), and the locator, which corresponds to the pattern of the verb.

In these pages, we have attempted to show, however briefly and perhaps clumsily, in what ways Sībawayhi's originality consisted in the Arabic tradition. We are perfectly conscious that our hypothesis still needs further discussion and many readjustments in order to be really adequate. We are also conscious that it raises many problems, notably that of accounting for the indisputable continuity between Sībawayhi and the classical grammarians. But we feel that such problems can only be treated by a careful study of the transmission and reception of the *Kitāb* in the different periods of the Arabic tradition. Moreover, it should be stressed that while Sībawayhi's originality appears mostly in the syntactico-semantic level, his morpho-phonology and morpho-syntax (i.e., notably, all that concerns the more formal aspects of the distribution of case markers) are basically identical to that of the later grammarians. As these were more directly interested in these two formal aspects of grammatical analysis, it can be understood that they failed to perceive what was most original in the *Kitāb*.

3

THE CANONICAL THEORY OF GRAMMAR: SYNTAX (*NAḤW*)

This chapter and the next one will be devoted to what can be considered as the two central fields of the Arabic linguistic tradition: syntax (*ʿilm al-naḥw*, *ʿilm al-iʿrāb*) and morpho-phonology (*ʿilm al-taṣrīf*), such as they were expounded within what we have defined as thc 'canonical' theoretical framework. This central position is measured not so much in terms of 'universal' relevance or interest (since we can quite legitimately feel that text linguistics or grammatical semantics are at least as important from this point of view) as it is in terms of enduring social and intellectual influence on the overall cultural system of Classical Islam. By then, a thorough knowledge of grammar (in the restrictive sense of morpho-phonology and syntax) was considered as a fundamental prerequisite for any other intellectual pursuit, religious or secular. Everybody who had any kind of cultural pretension was expected not only to know how to apply the basic rules of grammar so as to avoid gross errors, but they were also supposed to be able to expound articulately the most difficult points of grammatical theory, and to apply it to the most complex and recondite kinds of data.

This social function of grammar, as both fundamental teaching matter and imaginary barrier distinguishing the cultivated 'elite' from the 'vulgar', was not without theoretical influence. While there was no objection in principle to the grammarians' indulging in disinterested speculation, the kind of theory they were expected to evolve ought primarily to answer to the needs of the society they lived in. It had, more specifically, to provide an effective, workable solution to the difficulties encountered by learners, who usually knew some form or other of vernacular Arabic, in mastering the most characteristic features of *kalām al-ʿArab*, that is those which were considered as distinguishing 'Classical' Arabic from the vernacular.

In so far as syntax was concerned, the most important of these features was incontestably the use of case and mood markers (*iʿrāb*). This goes towards explaining how the theory of government, the aim of which was precisely to account for the distribution of *iʿrāb* marks, came to have a central position within the theory, while getting more and more formalized in the process. From a didactic point of view, it could seem much more expedient to teach a set of mechanical rules supposed to operate in any circumstance, than to take into account elements which were felt to be less easy to formalize, notably those which related to the enunciative aspect of language, which, as we saw in the preceding chapter, seem to have played an important part in Sībawayhi's approach. But on the other hand, the classical theory of government still allowed space for disinterested theoretical speculation, as it offered a way in which the syntactic relations between the components of the utterance could be expressed in a quite general and abstract way. That is why the two aspects of grammar, didactic and speculative, coexisted for such a long time within the tradition. They coexisted, moreover, not as two distinct subtraditions, but as two levels of the same theory.

In this chapter we shall be concerned mainly with the scholarly or speculative level, such as it is expressed by the most representative grammarians of the sixth/twelfth and seventh/thirteenth centuries, in whom the formal approach to syntax initiated by the fourth/tenth-century masters reached its apex.

BASIC CONCEPTS

Parts of speech

Not very surprisingly, the first chapter of any grammatical treatise is usually devoted to the parts of speech, or, to use the exact terminology, the 'kinds of words' (*al-kalim*): namely, the noun (*ism*), the verb (*fiʿl*), and the particle (*ḥarf*). As a matter of fact, this custom harks back to Sībawayhi's *Kitāb*. However, the contents of this chapter can vary considerably between one treatise and another. Didactic grammars (such as the commentaries on the *Alfiyya* or Ibn Hišām's shorter treatises) commonly limit themselves to enumerating, for each category, a list of characteristic properties (usually morphological or morpho-syntactic) enabling the learner to assign any unknown word to its proper category. As for more theoretically oriented treatises, they endeavour to give a formal scientific (according to the criteria of the period) definition of each category, and to establish the general system on a rational basis, by 'proving' that no other is logically conceivable.

These discussions, however, are of mainly academic interest: their only aim is to legitimate a pre-existent system on an *a posteriori* basis, without changing it in the least. As a matter of fact, there never was any disagreement between grammarians on the general principles (see J.-P. Guillaume, 1988). This remarkable consistency (as opposed to the chronic instability exhibited on the same question by the occidental tradition) can be partly explained by the simplicity and generality of the system, which could quite easily pass into other language-oriented disciplines, such as rhetoric and grammatical semantics, but also *uṣūl al-fiqh*, Qur'ānic exegesis, and theology. Besides, it was accompanied by a set of procedures which guaranteed its adequacy to the multiplicity and variety of the empirical data. These procedures, closely related to what we have called the 'integrative logic' of *qiyās*, enabled the Arabic tradition to escape the dilemma recurrent within occidental linguistic thought from classical times onwards: either to reduce the number of categories in order to enhance the generality of the system; or, inversely, to multiply them so as to match more closely the empirical data.

The fact that the parts of speech form a closed system (since any word necessarily belongs to one class, and to one only) further enhances the efficiency of the 'integrative' approach. It becomes possible to distinguish, in each category, besides the 'hard core' (the *aṣl* or *bāb*) exhibiting all of its characteristic properties, two 'margins', consisting of one or more subclasses which, through their particular behaviour, can be compared with one of the remaining categories. This 'likening' or 'formal assimilation' (*tašbīh*) is made on the basis of a bundle of properties of the concerned subclass, all of which represent a 'deviance' from the normal behaviour of the class (identified with the behaviour of the 'hard core'). These properties usually relate to different levels of analysis (morphological, morpho-syntactic, distributional, semantic). In this way, it is possible to account for each one of these 'deviant' properties in terms of the 'similarity' between the subclass to which they belong and another category, this similarity being further argumented by referring to the other properties.

The greatest number of such deviant subcategories appear, rather predictably, in the case of the noun. Besides the 'hard core', that is the substantive (*ism al-ǧins, ism al-ʿayn*), it comprises two 'margins', one related to the verb and one related to the particle. The latter consists mainly of the different kinds of pronouns (personal, demonstrative, interrogative). This assimilation is based upon both formal and semantic considerations: formally, pronouns have in common with particles that they take neither case nor determination marks (actually, of course, they are determinate by nature); and, semantically, they have no meaning in themselves but signify in something else, as particles do. In modern terminology, we would say that they have no meaning but only sense effects (see Ibn Yaʿīš, *Šarḥ al-Mufaṣṣal*, III: 80; 84; 126; 137). On the same side, but nearer to the noun, are the 'circumstants' (*ẓurūf*), nouns designating abstract spatial and temporal relationships which, because of their particular meanings, are used much in the same way as prepositions, such as *amāma* ('before') or *ʿinda* ('at, near by').

Related to the verb are to be found several classes of 'verbo-nominal' elements such as the *maṣdar* (i.e. the name of the verbal notion considered independently of its instantiation), the active and passive participles, and some classes of adjectives, which all have in common that, like the verb and unlike the hard-core substantives, they can govern the nominative and accusative. The most typical case is that of the active participle (*ism al-fāʿil*, literally 'the name of the doer'), which can assign accusative marking to the object of the process, but only when it has the meaning of the imperfect: besides *ḍāribu Zaydin* ('hitter-nom. Zayd-gen.', i.e. 'the one who has hit Zayd'), where the participle has its nominal value, one can have *al-ḍāribu Zaydan* ('the-hitter-nom. Zayd-acc.', i.e. 'the one who is presently hitting Zayd'), or even *ḍāribun Zaydan* ('one who is hitting Z.'), where it has its verbal value. Moreover, the morphological structure of the active participle, according to the grammarians, exhibits a basic similarity with that of the imperfect verb, *yafʿal*, as shown in this diagram (for the status of *alif*, notated here as ", see below, p. 99 n.3).

f	a	"	ʿ	i	l
|	|	|	|	|	|
y	a	f	ʿ	a	l
C	V	C	C	V	C

Lastly, the use of the active participle and, for that matter, the qualificative adjectives, is somewhat more restricted than the use of the 'true' nouns. For instance, they cannot very well function as subject of a verbal sentence when they are undetermined, e.g. *qāma ğamīlun* ('a handsome stood up', for 'a handsome man stood up'). According to Sībawayhi, such a sentence is, if not downright unacceptable, at least awkward (*ḍaʿīf*). On the other hand, participles and adjectives can very well be used as predicates of a nominal sentence, such as *Zaydun ğamīlun* ('Z. is handsome'). Now, according to the Arabic grammarians, this behaviour closely parallels that of the verb, which is always predicate of the sentence and never predicand.

The same similarity between the active participle and the verb is also used with respect to the verb, in order to account for the fact that the final vowel of the imperfect is subject to variation (corresponding to mood marking), a phenomenon which the Arabic grammarians assimilate to the case markings of the noun. The arguments for this comparison are the same, only the explanation goes the other way round. Symmetrically, there are several categories of verbs which are likened to particles: the exclamative verbs, such as *bi'sa* ('how bad') and *niʿma* ('how good'), which have no inflection whatsoever, and exhibit a nonverbal radical CiCC. The second main subclass of particle-like verbs are the aspectual auxiliaries of the *kāna* class, called by the later tradition 'deficient verbs' (*nawāqiṣ*), as they signify only a time, while true verbs signify both a time and a process. Their case is likened to the modal particles of the *inna* class, as they also affect a nominal predication.

A residual category (it is often defined as 'what is neither noun nor verb'), the particle, comprises only one margin, on the verb's side: it consists in the *inna* class, which, as we saw earlier, governs both predicand and predicate of a nominal sentence, while 'normal' particles either have no government or govern one element only. For this reason, the particles of the *inna* class are likened to the *kāna* class auxiliary verbs. Here again, the circularity of the system goes for greater strength and generality.

Iʿrāb and *binā'*

Immediately after the chapter devoted to the parts of speech there is, in nearly every treatise, a chapter analysing the contrasting pair formed by the notions of *iʿrāb* and *bināʾ*. The former is classically defined as 'the variation of the final vowel in words after their insertion in the utterance, and determined by the different governing operators (*ʿawāmil*) which affect them'; the latter is simply defined as the absence of such a variation. *Iʿrāb* can be observed in two cases: the noun, where it corresponds to a system of case markers; and the imperfect verb, where it corresponds to a system of mood markers, as can be seen from the chart provided here.

Vowel	u	a	i	∅
Technical term	rafʿ	naṣb	ǧarr	ǧazm
Noun	nominative	accusative	genitive	∅
Verb	indicative	subjunctive	∅	jussive

Actually, there are several other systems for the spelling of case markers, which appear in particular cases; their enumeration, which would be pointless here, occupies considerable space in most treatises.

As is apparent from this chart, the Arabic tradition uses the same terms to denote both nominal cases and verbal moods. For the classical grammarians, however, these two categories are not put on the same level. The prevailing idea is that the function of *iʿrāb* is to mark the several semantic values (*maʿānī*) which can affect an element by its insertion in an utterance. But then, this function, according to the grammarians, is only fulfilled in the case of the noun, where it helps to distinguish between the subject and the object of the verbal sentence. The topical argument is that, if there were no *iʿrāb*, an utterance such as *ḍaraba ʿAmr Zayd* ('hit Z. A.') would either be ambiguous, since there would be no way to know who hit whom, or interpretable through word ordering only, since the subject normally precedes the object; but in the latter case, speakers would lack all freedom to modify the 'canonical' word ordering, which would be quite inconvenient, notably in poetry. Accordingly, the nominative is claimed to be intrinsically the mark of the subject (*fāʿil*) and the accusative the mark of the object (*mafʿūl bi-hi*); all their other uses (such as the theme and predicate of the nominal sentence, or the accusative after the exceptive particle *illā*) being considered as 'secondary' and derived from the basic ones. As for the genitive, it was identified for the sake of coherence as the mark of the 'annexion' (*iḍāfa*), a rather vague term usually designating the (mainly) formal relationship between the noun and its complement (see al-Zağğāğī, *Īḍāḥ*: 69ff.; Ibn Ya'īš, *Šarḥ al-Mufaṣṣal*, I: 72f.).

Now, the classical grammarians argued that such a systematic relation between *i'rāb* marks and semantic values did not obtain in the case of the imperfect verb; they concluded, accordingly, that the verbal *i'rāb* was simply a 'formal' (as opposed to semantic) phenomenon, which could be adequately accounted for by the equally formal 'likeness' between the imperfect verb and the active participle, and described by listing the several elements which can govern the verb, and mentioning the kind of mark they assign to it. Such a decision, actually, is rather symptomatic of the Arabic tradition's lack of interest in the semantics of the verbal system, which was never approached in a systematic way.

Sentence and utterance

Besides the parts of speech and case-marker system, in which consists the conceptual backbone of the syntactic theory, an important number of treatises devote a chapter of their prolegomena to the notion of 'utterance' (*kalām*). In the didactic treatises, this discussion is usually very short, and confined to the statement that the minimal utterance is composed of two elements joined together by a predicative relationship (*isnād*), these elements being either two nouns, such as *Zaydun axū-ka* ('Z. is thy brother'), or a verb and a noun such as *qāma Zaydun* ('Z. stood up'). More scholarly treatises, on the other hand, devote longer developments to a more precise analysis of the notion of *isnād*, and of the difference between 'utterance' (*kalām*) and 'sentence' (*ğumla*).

The use of the term *isnād* in the meaning of 'predicative relationship' seems to have become generally accepted only at a rather late period. We have seen that it does not appear in Sībawayhi's *Kitāb*, although he uses, sporadically, the etymologically related terms of *musnad* and *musnad ilay-hi*. As for Ibn al-Sarrāğ, he seems to prefer terms derived from the roots XBR (*muxbar 'an-hu, xabar*) or ḤDṮ (*muḥaddaṯ 'an-hu, ḥadīṯ*) (also used by Sībawayhi), even if other fourth/tenth-century grammarians usually used *isnād* and its derivatives. As far as we know, however, it is only from the sixth/twelfth century onwards that some grammarians, such as Ibn Ya'īš (*Šarḥ al-Mufaṣṣal*, I: 20) or al-Astarābāḏī (*Kāfiya*, I: 8f.), begin to distinguish explicitly between the notion of *xabar*, which refers to a constative predication, and the more general notion of *isnād*, which also comprehends non-constative predications. However, the number and nature of these 'speech acts' vary considerably between one author and another. While Ibn Ya'īš only mentions, besides constation or 'information' (*xabar*), order (*amr*), prohibition (*nahy*), and interrogation (*istifhām*), al-Astarābāḏī, on an altogether more perceptive basis, mentions performation (*inšā'*), request (*ṭalab*, which includes order, prohibition, and optation), but also cases of non-asserted or pre-asserted predication, notably those which are implicit in the *maṣdar* and in the active and passive participles.

The distinction between *kalām* and *ǧumla* also took some time to become fully evolved. While it is ignored by Sībawayhi, the term *ǧumla* appears in al-Mubarrad's *Muqtaḍab* (I: 8), but it is not clear whether he intends by it something different from what Sībawayhi means by *kalām*. A century later, Ibn Ǧinnī seems at first glance to use the two terms interchangeably when he says: '*kalām* means any semantically independent sequence of sounds: that is what grammarians call "sentences" (*ǧumal*, plur. of *ǧumla*)' (*Xaṣā'iṣ*, I: 17); but then he adds two pages further: '*kalām* are those sentences which are independent in themselves, and do not need anything else' (ibid.: 19): this seems to exclude, at least implicitly, 'dependent' sentences, i.e. subordinate clauses. The same ambiguity can still be found in Zamaxšarī's *Mufaṣṣal* and its commentary by Ibn Ya'īš, as *kalām*, according to the latter, is the common 'genus', the 'species' of which are respectively the 'nominal' and 'verbal' sentences (*ǧumla ismiyya, ǧumla fi'liyya*). On the other hand, al-Astarābāḏī draws a neat distinction between *kalām*, which is intended as a semantically independent utterance, and *ǧumla*, which can be used for any sentence, whether it be independent or not: 'any *kalām* is a *ǧumla*, but not the reverse'.

As a matter of fact, it seems that the distinction between the two terms does not depend so much on the kind of linguistic sequence to which they can refer as on the way in which this sequence is considered: what characterizes *kalām* is the fact that it bears a single load of information (*fā'ida*), to the realization of which all the constitutive elements of the sequence contribute; while *ǧumla* suggests a more formalistic approach, taking into account the nature of these elements and their structural relationships. That is why it is possible to speak of *ǧumla ismiyya* or *fi'liyya* (nominal and verbal sentences), while no grammarian, to our knowledge, ever uses the expression *kalām fi'lī* or *ismī*. Moreover, *ǧumla*, whether it is independent or not, is the maximal domain in which operates the basic syntactic analytical device evolved by the Arabic tradition: namely, the theory of government, as we shall see presently.

THE THEORY OF GOVERNMENT

General principles

While they are never formally laid down by any treatises, the general principles of the theory are quite often referred to in discussions about empirical cases. For the sake of clarity, we will briefly state them here as they were accepted by most classical grammarians.

1 Any *i'rāb* mark exhibited by a noun or an (imperfect) verb in a sentence is assigned by an 'operation' (*'amal*) performed by another element of the same sentence, whether it be independent or not.

2 This 'operating element' or 'governing operator' (*'āmil*) must necessarily occur before its operand (*ma'mūl fī-hi*) in the canonical (i.e. unmarked) order of the sentence; the order can be later changed, under specific conditions, by transfer rules (*taqdīm wa-ta'xīr*, literally 'anteposition and postposition'). For instance, on the basis of a 'canonical' verbal sentence such as *ḍaraba Zaydun 'Amran* (''Amr hit Zayd'), where the verb *ḍaraba* successively assigns the nominative to the subject, *Zayd*, and the accusative to the object, *'Amr*, it is possible to derive *ḍaraba 'Amran Zaydun* and *'Amran ḍaraba Zaydun* by transfer of the object. On the other hand, the anteposition of the subject brings about a complete change in the syntactic structure of the sentence: while *Zaydun ḍaraba 'Amran* is perfectly correct, in this case *Zaydun* is no more analysed as an 'anteposed subject', but as the 'theme' (*mubtada'*) of

a nominal sentence, governed by the *ibtidā'* (see below, p. 60).

3 A given element can never govern another element belonging to its own category: a verb cannot govern a verb, neither can a noun govern a noun (except in the case of the verbo-nominals; see below, p. 59). A given element can only govern elements belonging to the same category.

4 Government only operates on the head of a verb or noun phrase; the *iʿrāb* mark is later assigned on the head's 'dependencies' (*tawābiʿ*), in so far as they can receive such a mark. The 'dependencies' of the noun are the epithet (*naʿt*), the apposition (*badal*), the corroborative (*tawkīd*), the specificative (*ʿaṭf bayān*), and the coordinated noun or nouns (*maʿṭūf*); the only dependency of the verb is the coordinated verb or verbs.

Some classical treatises devote considerable space to the discussion of the metalinguistic status of the notion of *ʿamal*. As far back as the fourth/tenth century, grammarians such as al-Zağğāğī and Ibn Ğinnī (and probably others too) took pains to stress that, when grammarians say that 'such a word operates on such another', they do not mean that it actually does something to it, as words, being only sequences of articulated sounds produced by the phonatory organs, cannot act upon each other as bodies do. The use of the term *ʿamal* must be understood metaphorically, as a 'convention' (*iṣṭilāḥ*) specific to the grammarians' technical usage (*awḍāʿ al-naḥwiyyīn*): properly, the assignation of *iʿrāb* marks is an act of the speaker. This clarification was, actually, only a part of a wider movement, perceptible in many contemporary grammatical works, by which the grammatical metalanguage became explicitly and systematically distinguished from ordinary language. But, whereas such a statement was perfectly commonplace in the fourth/tenth century, when most thinkers were under the influence of the Muʿtazilite school of thought, it became somewhat embarrassing after the mid-fifth/eleventh-century 'Sunni restoration' brought about the triumph of Ašʿarism as the majority expression of Islam, as, for consistent Ašʿarites, only God can be qualified as 'acting', and not a human speaker.

This point was raised notably by the Andalusian grammarian Ibn Maḍā' (d. 1208), who, in his *Radd* ('The Refutation of Grammarians') categorically rejects the notion of *ʿamal* as heresy;

but this rejection remains at a merely verbal level, as he concludes by advocating the use of *taʿalluq* (dependence) in practically the same sense. This suggestion, however, was never accepted, and the tradition as a whole followed a more conservative solution, which enabled them to keep the litigious terminology while reinterpreting it in a theologically harmless way. According to one of the main representatives of this 'middle way', Abū l-Barakāt al-Anbārī, the so-called 'operators' (*ʿawāmil*, plur. of *ʿāmil*) must be considered not as affecting in an actually physical way the elements they operate upon, but only as 'marks' or 'pointers' (*ʿalāmāt*), enabling the speakers to assign the correct endings to nouns and verbs; in other words, there is no material relationship between the operator and its operand, only a conventional link.

The governing operators

As we saw, the fact that an element can govern another (or, conversely, can be governed by it) is determined by the part of speech it belongs to. It is on such a basis that the treatises expound the general rules of the system.

The noun, by definition, is always submitted to another element's government; on the other hand, according to the majority opinion, it has not the capacity to govern anything. It should be noted here that this decision entails a rather complex analysis in order to account for the assignation of the genitive to the adnominal complement (see below, p. 63). As for the government exercised by verbo-nominals such as the *maṣdar*, participles, and participial adjectives, it is attributed to the verbal notion (*maʿnā l-fiʿl*) which is implicit in them.

The verb is the governing element *par excellence*, as it necessarily assigns at least the nominative to the noun which immediately follows it (in the unmarked case, its 'subject' or 'doer', *fāʿil*), and the accusative to all the nouns which occur after that, whenever they are not already governed by another element (e.g. a preposition). When the verb is in the imperfect, it can also be governed by several particles, which assign it either the subjunctive or the jussive. A verb not governed by any such particle is in the indicative, the unmarked mood. However, the logic of the system (no *iʿrāb* mark without a governing element) induced the grammarians to try and identify also in this case, an element which assigns the indicative to the verb. According to the majority, it is an 'abstract operator' (*ʿāmil maʿnawī*; see below), that is a phonetically void element, identified by the fact that the verb occurs in a position which can be occupied by a noun. For instance, in *yaqūmu Zaydun* ('Z. is standing up'), *yaqūmu* occurs in a position where one could also find the active participle, *qā'imun Zaydun* ('He's standing up, Z.').

As for the particle, it does not necessarily govern (contrary to the verb), but some particles can (contrary to the noun). Among the latter, some can govern verbs, assigning to them either the subjunctive or the jussive, while the others govern nouns, assigning them either the genitive (in the case of prepositions) or the accusative (in the case of some negative and exceptive particles). We have already mentioned the case of the *inna*-class particles, which govern two nouns.

There is, lastly, a fourth category of governing element, the 'abstract operator' (*ʿāmil maʿnawī*), characterized by the fact that it is phonetically void. The most important and representative kind of *ʿāmil maʿnawī* is the *ibtidā'*, which assigns the nominative to the theme (*mubtada'*) and predicate of the nominal sentence. For the most consistent classical grammarians, *ibtidā'* is defined in a drastically formalistic way, as the lack of any phonetically representable governing element, which amounts to a governing element devoid of phonetical representation. Some treatises, however, use expressions relating to it which suggest Sībawayhi's more enunciative approach; these expressions, however, have no longer any precise theoretical status within the formal syntax evolved by the classical tradition.

Abstractness in the theory of government

The highly formalized character of the system and the great generality of the case-assignment rules often make it necessary for the grammarians to use abstract analyses in order to process adequately some classes of data. These analyses, generally speaking, imply the reconstruction of an underlying form (*taqdīr*) exhibiting an element both absent from the actual form and crucial to account for the data. This reconstructed element can be either an *iʿrāb* mark which, for some reason, cannot appear in the actual form but can be deduced at an abstract level from the status of the term in the syntactical structure of the sentence; or it can be a governing element lacking from the actual form, while its presence is necessary to account for the distribution of *iʿrāb* marks within the sentence.

Statutory *iʿrāb* (*iʿrāb maḥallī*)

This notion actually covers two rather different kinds of facts, according to whether it relates to an isolated term (noun or verb) or to a dependent sentence. The former concerns the nouns which do not exhibit distinctive *iʿrāb* marks, either because they are by nature undeclinable (e.g. demonstrative or relatives), or by the play of morpho-phonological constraints. In this case, the nature of the abstract *iʿrāb* mark will be figured out on the basis of the status (*maḥall*) of the word within the sentence. For instance, in *hāḏā Zaydun* ('This is Z.'), the demonstrative *hāḏā* is 'statutorily' in the nominative, since it is the theme of a nominal sentence.

Dependent sentences are formally assimilated to nouns, as they occur in the same places as nouns do. For instance, in *Zaydun abū-hu qā'imun* ('Z., his father is standing'), the nominal sentence *abū-hu qā'imun* is analysed as the predicate of the 'greater sentence' (*al-ǧumla al-kubrā*), of which it is a part, exactly as the noun *munṭaliqun* would be in *Zaydun munṭaliqun* ('Z. is going away'); accordingly, it is analysed as statutorily in the nominative (*marfūʿ maḥallan*). While the general principle underlying this kind of analysis is quite straightforward, its practical application can sometimes raise difficult problems, as in many cases there is no formal mark enabling one to decide at first glance whether a sentence is independent or not. Consequently, there are many cases when two different analyses for the same utterance can coexist. For instance, in *Zaydun munṭaliqun wa-abū-hu qā'imun* ('Z. is going away and his father is standing up') the second sentence, *wa-abū-hu qā'imun*, can be analysed either as coordinate with the first, in which case it must be considered as independent (and, consequently, as having no statutory *iʿrāb*), or as coordinate with the predicate of the first, in which case it will be considered as dependent and statutorily in the nominative, the underlying analysis being something like *Zaydun munṭaliqun wa-Zaydun abū-hu qā'imun* ('Z. is going away and Z., his father is standing'). In this specific instance the ambiguity is, admittedly, of a minor kind, but in other, more difficult cases different analyses can hold for quite different semantic interpretations.

Quite predictably, it is in the field of text linguistics, and in particular in Qur'ānic exegesis, that this kind of problem was most constantly raised, and produced most sophisticated discussions. However, it usually occupies a quite minor position in grammatical treatises, since it is only evoked through local discussions about points of detail; the reason being that the grammarians' approach usually remained within the bounds of the sentence. But rather later, some writers devoted whole chapters to the question, bringing together data and arguments which, until then, had remained scattered in grammatical treatises as well as in exegetical works. The most important text in this field is the second part of Ibn Hišām's *Muḡnī l-Labīb*.

Taqdīr al-iʿrāb

The second manifestation of abstractness in syntactic analysis occurs whenever an element exhibits an *iʿrāb* mark in the absence of any governing operator (whether phonetically full or not) liable to assign it. In this case it is necessary to reconstruct an abstract representation of the sentence (*taqdīr*) where the distribution of *iʿrāb* marks can be affected normally, then to elide (*ḥaḏf*) from this abstract form the surplus element or elements (i.e. those which do not appear in the actual sentence). This elision, moreover, should normally be motivated on grounds of principle.

In the most straightforward kind of case, the motivation is that the elided element is redundant due to some other element in the context. For instance, if a speaker answers the question *Man ra'ayta?* ('Whom did you see?') by saying *Zaydan* ('Z.-acc.'), the presence of the accusative in *Zaydan* will be explained by reconstructing an abstract representation, *ra'aytu Zaydan* ('I saw Z.-acc.'), where the verb *ra'aytu* regularly assigns the accusative to *Zaydan*, and by subsequently eliding this verb on the grounds that it is already present in the immediate context (*ḥaḏf li-sabq al-wurūd*). Another, not very different case occurs when the extralinguistic situation makes the explicit mention of the verb useless (*ḥaḏf li-dalālat al-ḥāl*); for instance, if a speaker, seeing somebody shooting with a bow, exclaims *Al-qirṭāsa wallāh!* ('The mark-acc. by God!'), the 'elided' verb being, of course, *aṣabta* ('you hit').

In other cases, the reconstruction of the abstract form can

appear less intuitively evident, and widely different from the common-sense paraphrase of the sentence concerned. Ibn Ǧinnī, for instance, stresses that in an utterance such as *ahla-ka wa-l-layla* ('Your kin-acc. and the night-acc.'), it is necessary to distinguish between the semantic paraphrase (*tafsīr al-maʿnā*), which would give something like *ilḥaq ahla-ka qabla l-layli* ('Catch up with your kin before the night'), and the technical *taqdīr* (*taqdīr al-iʿrāb*), which is *ilḥaq ahla-ka wa-sbiqi l-layla* ('Catch up with your kin and overtake the night'). Although this utterance does not seem very natural, it enables one to account for the accusative in *al-layla*, which the first paraphrase evidently could not.

In other cases, the reconstructed abstract representation can even be an unattestable utterance, or an utterance attestable only with a different meaning. An instance of the first can be found in the traditional analysis of utterances such as *Zaydan ḍarabtu-hu* ('Z.-acc., I hit him'), where the accusative in *Zaydan* cannot be accounted for by the government of the verb *ḍarabtu*, since it is already exercised on the anaphorical pronoun *-hu*. The abstract representation is accordingly reconstructed as *ḍarabtu Zaydan ḍarabtu-hu*, where the second occurrence of *ḍarabtu* is analysed as a 'corroborative' (*ta'kīd*) of the first; after having assigned the accusative to *Zaydan*, the first occurrence of the verb is elided on the grounds that it is made redundant by the second. As for cases where the reconstructed form has a different meaning from the surface one, they are most typically exemplified by the analysis of the assignment of genitive to the adnominal complement, that is what the Semitists usually call 'annexion' (*iḍāfa*), such as *ǧulāmu Zaydin* ('page-boy Zayd-gen.', i.e. 'Z.'s page-boy'). As the theory explicitly precludes a noun directly governing another one, and postulates, moreover, that prepositions are the only kind of elements able to assign the genitive to a noun, it is necessary to reconstruct an abstract representation containing a preposition, such as *ǧulāmun li-Zaydin* ('a page-boy [belonging] to Z.-gen.'). In other kinds of 'annexions', the underlying preposition will be identified with *min* ('of, from') or *fī* ('in, at'). But, in this case, the elision of the preposition will furthermore give to the first noun a value of determination (*taʿrīf*) which it did not have in the abstract representation, as *ǧulāmu Zaydin* means 'Z.'s page-boy' and not 'a page-boy of Z.'s'.

GOVERNMENT AND PREDICATION

The two models

The general economy of the government theory leads to a distinction between local government, effected by an operator (usually a particle) on a single element, and global government, where a single element (paradigmatically a verb) effects the distribution of *iʿrāb* marks on all the other components of the sentence. Although this difference is never actually stated by the grammarians, it is nevertheless strongly suggested by (among others) their belief that every prepositional phrase (*ǧārr wa-maǧrūr*) is statutorily in the accusative, since it is a sentence specifier governed by a verb or a verb-like element.

In its most transparent and paradigmatic form, the model of global government is represented by the canonical verbal sentence, where the verb in the leading position successively assigns the nominative to the subject, and the accusative to the object (and, actually, to all the other nominal components of the sentence):

(1) *Verb* ḍaraba — *Subject* Zaydun — *Object* ʿAmran

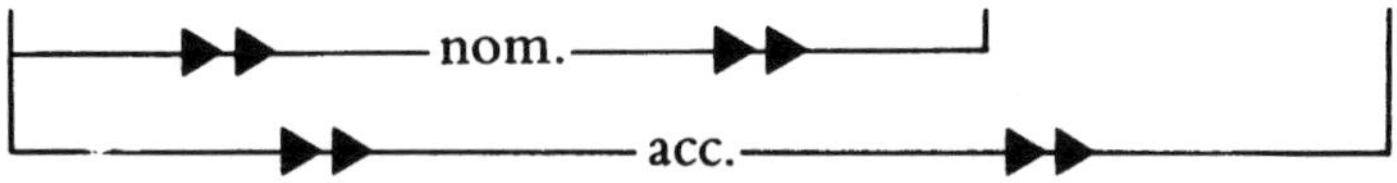

(ʿZ. hit ʿAmr')

The very nature of the data dictate a ternary model, with a governing element and two governed ones, each one being affected with a distinctive mark correlated with its semantico-syntactic function within the sentence. As we saw earlier, the classical grammarians applied the same model to the analysis of the nominal sentence, where the *ibtidā'*, represented by a void element (∅), has the same function as the verb in (1):

(2) *Ibtidā'* ∅ — *Mubtada'* Zaydun — *Xabar* munṭaliqun

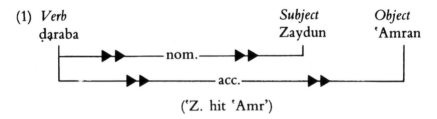

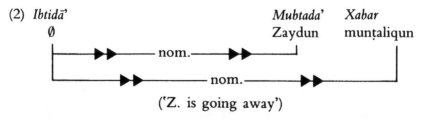

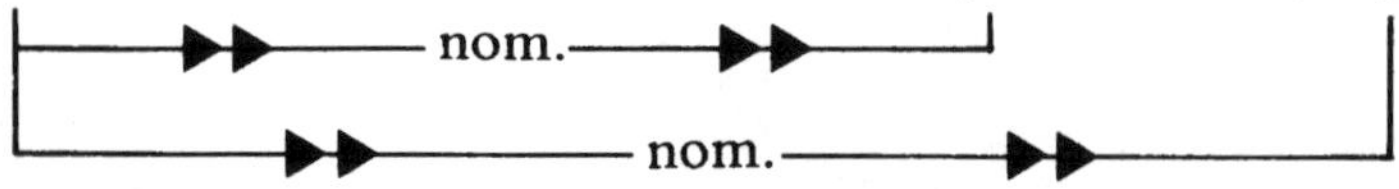

('Z. is going away')

This analysis is further reinforced by the fact that it can account in a systematic, if utterly formalistic, way for the fact that the *ibtidā'* can alternate with other elements which modify the distribution of case marks within the sentence while changing its aspectual or modal value. These elements, which were at a rather late period gathered within the general category of *nawāsix al-ibtidā'* ('abrogators of *ibtidā'*'), comprise the aspectual auxiliary verbs of the *kāna* class, the modal particles of the *inna* class, and the 'epistemic' verbs of the *ẓanna* class:

(3) 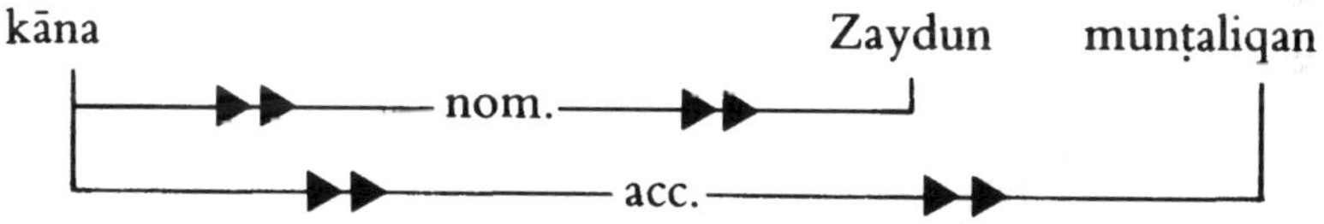

('Z. was going away')

(4) 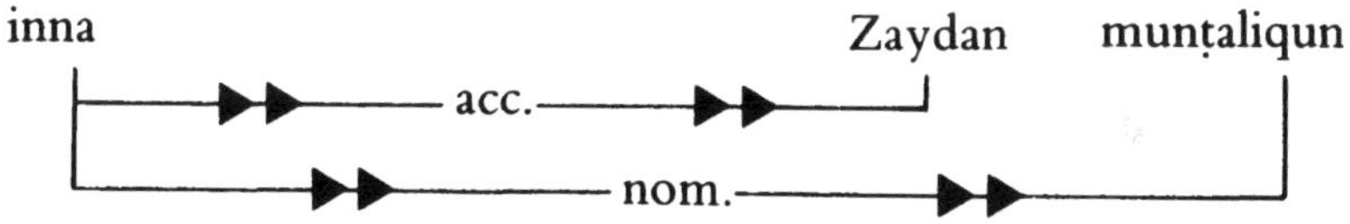

('Here is Z. He is going away')

(5) 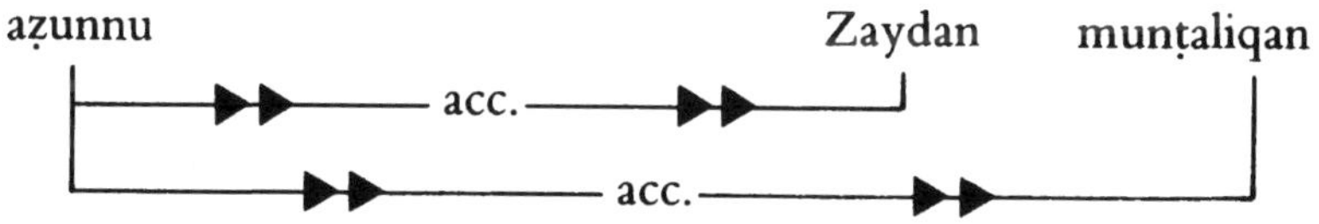

('I believe (that) Z. (is) going away')

As for the predicative model, it relies on a binary pattern, distinguishing, at a first level, between the predicative elements of the sentence (*'umad*, literally 'pillars') and the non-predicative elements (*faḍalāt*, literally 'surplus'); at a second level, a new binary distinction is made among the *'umad* between the predicand (*musnad ilay-hi*) and the predicate (*musnad*). It should be stressed that these logico-semantical categories do not directly correspond to syntactic ones, as the *musnad ilay-hi* can be realized either as a theme or a subject (according to whether it occurs in a nominal or a verbal sentence) and the *musnad* either as a predicate (*xabar*) or as a verb. The autonomy of these two levels of analysis is further enhanced by the fact the two kinds of sentences exhibit somewhat different formal structures, notably in what concerns word ordering.

Actually, the predicative model seems to apply most transparently to the nominal sentence (see (1) above), in so far as it shows an immediately recognizable binary structure, and, moreover, a predicand–predicate ordering, which, according to some grammarians, is the most 'normal', unmarked order. However, its application to the verbal sentence, while being neither impossible nor arbitrary, nevertheless necessitated some important theoretical decisions on the part of the grammarians. The most notable of these was to consider the markings of person on the verb as pronouns; for instance, an utterance like *šaribtu* ('I drank') is analysed as a conjugated verb, *šariba*, and the first-person masculine singular pronoun *-tu*, exactly as *šariba Zaydun* ('Z. drank'). In this system, the pronoun of the third-person singular has a peculiar status, since it corresponds to a phonetically void element, the 'masked pronoun' (*al-ḍamīr al-mustatir*), which is in complementary distribution with full nouns. Hence, *qāma* ('he stood up') will be analysed as *qāma–δ*, where *δ* stands for the *ḍamīr mustatir*, which has exactly the same function as *Zaydun* in *qāma Zaydun*. In the same way, *Zaydun qāma* ('Z., he stood up') will be analysed as a nominal sentence with *Zaydun* for theme, and for predicate a verbal sentence, the subject of which is a *ḍamīr mustatir* co-referent with *Zayd*. So the analysis of this sentence will be strictly identical with that of *Zaydun qāma abū-hu* ('Z. his father stood up'), where the place of the subject is occupied by a full name. In the same way, the presence of a *ḍamīr mustatir* was postulated in the 'implicit' verbal predications, that is those which are implied by the participles or participial adjectives. For instance, *qā'imun* in *rağulun qā'imun* ('a man standing up'), or *ğamīlun* in *rağulun ğamīlun* were analysed as *qā'imun–δ* and *ğamīlun–δ* respectively, since the position of *δ* can be occupied by a full name, as in *rağulun qā'imun abū-hu* ('a man standing his father', i.e. 'a man whose father is standing'), or *rağulun ğamīlun wağhu-hu* ('a man handsome his face', i.e. 'a handsome-faced man').

Another problem related to the application of the predicative model to the verbal sentence is that of the semantic link between the verb and its predicand (i.e., normally, the subject), but also between the verb and the other components of the sentence (the *faḍalāt*). The general idea expressed by many grammarians is that the verb is a semantically complex element, composed of several internal functions, and that every one of these can be specified by an element in the sentence. In order for there to be a verb or, more precisely, a 'doing', there must be a 'doer' (*fāʿil*), that is a subject, and a 'thing done' (*mafʿūl*), either as the process itself ('to hit' is 'to do a hitting'), which correspond to the internal object (*mafʿūl muṭlaq*) or as the object or objects affected by the process (one generally hits something or somebody), which corresponds to the external object (*mafʿūl bi-hi*), or both. Moreover, a doing necessarily happens in a specific time and place, to which correspond the 'circumstances' (*ẓurūf*). Lastly, to these intrinsic functions are added some others which have a less direct relationship to the process, such as the cause or motivation (*mafʿūl la-hu*), or the situation (*ḥāl*) in which the subject or the (external) object can be concomitants of the process.

In the classical theory, all these functions are 'signified' in a generic way by the verb, and can be specified by an element of the sentence. But for most grammarians this idea seems to be used only in order to explain the relationship between the verb and its complements; as Ibn al-Sarrāǧ has it: 'Generally speaking, the verb does not assign the accusative to an element unless it [i.e. the verb] contains an indication of it.' Such a formulation seems to exclude implicitly the element to which the verb assigns the nominative, that is the subject. There was, however, a place within the theory where this distinction, founded on purely formal criteria (subject = nominative and complements = accusative) was no longer relevant: the analysis of the passive verbal sentence, or, in Arabic terminology 'the doing whose doer is not named' (*fiʿl mā lā yusammā fāʿilu-hu*). In this case, the place of the subject in the active sentence, both as predicand and as the element bearing nominative marking, is occupied by a 'surrogate subject' (*nāʾib fāʿil*), corresponding to one of the following:

the external object, e.g. *ḍuriba Zaydun* ('Z. was hit');
the internal object, provided it is specified (*muxaṣṣaṣ*), either qualitatively, e.g. *ḍuriba ḍarbun šadīdun* ('A violent hitting was hit'), or quantitatively, e.g. *ḍuriba ḍarbatān* ('Two hits were hit');
the local circumstance (*ẓarf makān*), e.g. *sīra farsaxān* ('Two leagues were travelled');
the temporal circumstance (*ẓarf zamān*), e.g. *ṣīma Ramaḍānu* ('Ramadan was fasted').

While the didactic treatises limited themselves to listing all these possibilities, with a stress on the external object, which represents after all the most common occurrence, more theory-oriented grammarians tried to build a unified theory of the verbal predication so as to account both for the active and the different cases of passive sentences. Two distinct solutions were actually held: one by al-Zamaxšarī and his commentator Ibn Yaʿīš and the other by al-Astarābāḏī. The former's solution consists in redefining the category of *fāʿil* on a purely formalistic basis, as 'the predicand of a verb when it is postposed to this verb' (Ibn Yaʿīš, *Šarḥ al-Mufaṣṣal*, I: 74f.) which goes for the subject of the active sentence as well as for the different kinds of 'surrogate subjects' of the passive sentence. The latter's, which may seem more interesting, consists in finding a common semantic property subsuming all the elements which can be used as the predicand of a verbal sentence, whether active or passive. According to al-Astarābāḏī, all these elements have in common that they specify an intrinsic, 'necessary' dimension of the verbal notion (*ḍarūriyyāt al-fiʿl*); if the verb denotes a 'doing', it must necessarily involve a 'doer' (the subject), something 'done' (the internal object), somebody or something 'done to' (the external object), and a time and place when and where the doing is done (the circumstances). Consequently, the verb can accept any one of these as a predicand, even if there is at least a partial hierarchy between these elements (notably, whenever the 'doer' is expressed, it must necessarily be the predicand, and, in default of the 'doer', the external object). On the other hand, terms specifying less intrinsic or necessary dimensions of the verbal notion, such as the 'cause' or 'motivation', cannot be used as predicands of passive verbs, since, remarks al-Astarābāḏī, 'many an action is done with no cause at all'.

Two models or just one?

In nearly all the classical treatises, the models of government and predication are explicitly or implicitly considered as globally autonomous and irreducible. But then, this dichotomy seems to have been a comparatively late development, since the tradition keeps the traces of a period when the distinction was much less clear-cut. One of the most easily recognizable manifestations of this state of things is the existence of an alternative theory about the assignment of the nominative to the theme and predicate of the nominal sentence. Whereas, as we saw earlier, the classical analysis postulates the existence of a phonetically void element governing both elements, the 'Kūfan' theory of *tarāfuʿ* ('reciprocal assignment of the nominative) claims that the theme assigns its case to the predicate and vice versa. This analysis, in other terms, made crucial appeal to predicative considerations within the theory of government: what enabled the theme to govern the predicate, and vice versa, was the fact that they were joined by a predicative relationship.

It is also clear that the *tarāfuʿ* theory violated nearly all the basic principles of the theory of government; for this reason, it was attributed by classical grammarians to the 'Kūfan' school of grammar. That such an attribution (together with many others) is purely conventional is shown by the fact that Ibn al-Sarrāǧ himself (a Baṣran if there ever was) seems to use it without the least compunction. In his preliminary chapter, where he lays down the main principles of the theory of government, he cites among 'the cases where a noun can govern another noun [*sic*]' the theme and the predicate, saying in substance that the former is in the nominative because it is the 'point of departure' (*mubtada'*) on which the predicate is 'constructed' (*mabnī*), and the latter is also in the nominative because it is 'constructed' on the theme (*Uṣūl*, I: 52). It seems here as if the assignment of case marks did only reflect, on the formal, syntactico-semantic level, the semantic relation between the two terms 'by the combination of which the utterance is constituted and achieved' (*ya'talif bi-ǧtimāʿi-himā l-kalāmu wa-yatimm*; ibid.).

Now, it seems indisputable that this analysis is substantially equivalent to the *tarāfuʿ* theory attributed by later grammarians to the 'Kūfan school'. But then, if we read further on, we soon realize that things are somewhat more complex than that: some pages later, Ibn al-Sarrāǧ, treating in a more detailed fashion the problem of the assignment of nominative to the *mubtada'*, states without apparently seeing any contradiction with what he has formerly said: 'they [i.e. the *mubtada'* and the *xabar*] are both in the nominative; the *mubtada'* receives the nominative from the *ibtidā'*, and the *xabar* from both [i.e. the *ibtidā'* and the *mubtada'*]' (*Uṣūl*, I: 58), *ibtidā'* being explicitly assimilated to the lack of a phonetically realized governing element. In other words, it seems as if the two analyses which in later times will be crystallized into rival theories (the Kūfans' *tarāfuʿ* vs. the Baṣrans' *ibtidā'*) were still perceived as substantially equivalent and equally acceptable expressions of the same theory. We must, then, suppose that it is only in some later period that a stricter and more explicit elaboration of the theory of government caused the previous analysis to be perceived as inconsistent, and, accordingly, to be split into two antagonistic theories. Of these theories, the one which was in accordance with the current theoretical framework of syntax was naturally attributed to the Baṣran 'school', and the other, rejected one, to the Kūfans.

However, the dichotomy between the two models, predicative and governmental, was not so absolute that it precluded any attempt at finding analogies between the analyses they allowed. For instance, the idea is very often expressed that there is a regular correlation between the nominative and the predicative elements of the sentence (the *'umad*), and between the accusative and the non-predicative ones (the *faḍalāt*). But then, this idea remained in most cases confined to mere chance remarks devoid of any effective theoretical status; with a notable exception, no grammarian that we know of ever attempted to construct a unified system where the distribution of case marks would be directly accounted for on the basis of the theory of predication. The exception we alluded to is, once again, al-Astarābāḏī, incidentally the most brilliant and perceptive grammarian of the later classical period, on a page remarkable both for the lucidity and cogency of the reasoning and for the tactical cleverness of the argumentation.

The two theoretical obstacles standing in the way of a unified theory such as al-Astarābāḏī aimed at were, on one hand, the idea that the actual distribution of the *i'rāb* marks was governed, in its formal aspect, by the mechanics of the *'amal* and, on the other hand, the idea that its semantic aspect was adequately taken care of by saying that the nominative and the accusative were intrinsically the marks of, respectively, the subject and the object, their other uses being considered as secondary and derived. Al-Astarābāḏī's first step consists in refuting the latter, which certainly was the weakest of the two. Taking his departure from the current idea that the function of case marks is to discriminate the different semantic values which can affect a noun through its insertion in an utterance, he establishes that these values are only two: namely, the predicative or non-predicative character of the considered noun. The former corresponds to the nominative, the latter to the accusative in the most normal case, or, in some local configurations, the genitive. Having neatly tackled the first problem, he then addresses himself to the second. Once again taking his departure from what was, in his time, a quite commonplace idea, that the relation between the 'operating' (i.e. governing) element and the one on which it operates is purely conventional (i.e. not physical), he suggests that an alternative formulation of the same idea would be that the element which governs another is the element through which the governed element acquires both its semantic value as predicative or non-predicative and the corresponding marking, as these are indissociable. It is for this reason, he continues, that grammarians say that the verb governs its subject, since it is only through its relationship with the verb that the subject acquires its semantic value as a predicative element.

Up to now, al-Astarābāḏī's reasoning may appear only as a somewhat roundabout, but basically orthodox, way of expressing the common tenets of the classical tradition. But, after having most cleverly manoeuvred himself into a firm position, he suddenly passes to the attack, simply by applying to the nominal sentence exactly the same analysis that he has just used for the verbal sentence: since the theme only becomes a predicative element through the predicate, and vice versa, it follows logically that each one of them must be considered as governing the other, 'according to al-Kisāʾī and al-Farrāʾ', specifies al-Astarābāḏī, who naturally attributes this theory to its putative fathers, the two leading figures of the 'Kūfan' tradition. It is also to al-Farrāʾs authority that he appeals for his analysis of the accusative-assignment process to the *faḍalāt*: the governing element in this case is identified with the whole predicative nucleus, that is, normally, to the verb + subject group. He also mentions favourably the claim attributed to one Hišām ibn Muʿāwiya (a disciple of al-Kisāʾī's; Ibn Muʿāwiya died in 209/824) that the governor in this case is simply the subject: what seems interesting about this claim, says al-Astarābāḏī, is the fact that the subject 'saturates', so to speak, the predicative relationship opened by the verb and thus prevents the following elements from participating in it.

Al-Astarābāḏī's thesis (which should be compared with those of contemporary grammatical semantics, see Chap. 6) certainly made possible a drastic simplification of syntactical theory. It is interesting to note that, as far as we know, it was never accepted by any other grammarian. Of course, one should make allowance for the intellectual conservatism which was then dominating the most representative aspects of Islamic thought. But this is perhaps not the only reason which explains the survival of the classical dichotomy between the predicative and the governmental models: one should also take into account the weight of pedagogical constraints on the theory, which were always a constant in the development of the Arabic grammatical tradition. If what defines the social ends of grammar is to teach, among other things, the correct use of the case and mood endings, then the question needs to be asked whether al-Astarābāḏī's approach, whatever its theoretical merits, is a more appropriate means for this end than the formalist method, which consists (more or less) in listing the different kinds of governing elements together with instructions for their correct use. Actually, the advantage of the classical system is that the theory of government represents both its theoretical hard core *and* the apparatus through which grammar, or, in any case, syntax, achieves its specific socio-cultural programme; any attempt at removing it from its central position had few chances of success.

4

THE CANONICAL THEORY OF GRAMMAR: MORPHOLOGY, PHONOLOGY, AND PHONETICS (*TAṢRĪF*)

This part of grammar includes, for the AG, what we now call morphology, which defines the structure of words, phonology, which describes the variations within this structure, and phonetics, which is most often treated when studying one phonological process, gemination (*idġām*).

The division between two of the parts of this field, morphology and phonology, is perfectly explicit in the writings of the later grammarians. We find, for example, at the beginning of Ibn ʿUṣfūr's *Mumtiʿ*:

> *Taṣrīf* is comprised of two parts. The first consists in giving different forms to words in accordance with their various 'meanings' (*maʿnā*),[1] for example: *ḍaraba*, *ḍarraba*, *taḍarraba*, *taḍāraba*, *iḍṭaraba*.[2] Thus, from the word *ḍarb* comprised of *Ḍ*, *R*, *B*, such structures are derived for different 'meanings'; similarly, where the noun is concerned, the forms differ in accordance with the 'meanings' which affect it, such as the diminutive and the broken plural, examples: *zuyayd* ['little Zayd'] and *zuyūd* ['Zayd–s'].
>
> The second consists in changing the *aṣl* of the word, without this change indicating that the word is affected by a new 'meaning', as is the case for the change from *qawala* to *qāla*. It is clear that this change is not effected in order to indicate a 'meaning' different from that of *qawala* – the *aṣl* – if the latter were used.

Let us look, then, at the components of the two parts of *taṣrīf*.

MORPHOLOGY

Morphology enumerates the basic nominal and verbal structures (*binya aṣliyya*) and describes the processes of derivation which make it possible to generate from them other forms of the language. A basic structure is an arrangement of the positions of consonants and vowels linked with a grammatical 'meaning' (*ma'nā* II) (e.g. verb, past . . .). The positions of consonants and vowels are written F, ', and L: F=C1, first consonant; '=C2, second consonant; and L=C3, third consonant. The last of these is repeated to represent a fourth and, possibly, a fifth consonant. Thus CACC is written FA'L and CACCAC is written FA'LAL.

The segments of the root (*aṣl*) take their positions in the arrangements thus defined. The root itself is a complex element comprising two sides, one phonic (three or four consonants) and the other semantic (a semantic value common to all words which are derived from it, i.e. *ma'nā* I, see note 1).

No new words, except plurals and diminutives, can be regularly derived from the basic nominal structures (ten triconsonantal: FA'L, FI'L, FU'L, FA'AL, FA'IL, FA'UL, FI'AL, FI'IL, FU'UL, FU'AL; six quadriconsonantal: FA'LAL, FI'LIL, FU'LUL, FI'LAL, FI'ALL, FU'LAL; and four pentaconsonantal: FA'ALLAL, FI'LALL, FA'LALIL, FU'ALLIL). Hence, once their inventory is closed, they have been fully dealt with and we turn to the basic verbal forms (three triconsonantal: FA'ALA, FA'ILA and FA'ULA; and one quadriconsonantal: FA'LALA) which are the source of numerous morphological processes.

A preliminary question, which has been the subject of long controversies, concerns the way in which the association between the root and these basic verbal structures is effected. The prevailing opinion is that the association between the two is brought about by means of a nominal form (the *maṣdar*) which, by expressing a process without linking it to a given time is conceptually simpler than the verbal form, which is intrinsically linked with time, and constitutes the initial stage of all derivational processes.

Verbal morphology

The basic structures, which assume the form of the third person masculine of perfective verbs, e.g. *ḍaraba*, are involved in two types of processes: without augment and with augment. The first corresponds to what is traditionally called inflectional morphology, and the second to the morphology of derivation and composition.

1 Derivation 'without augment' does not modify the basic consonantal structure and makes it possible to derive the verbal form of the imperfect and of the imperative, by prefixation and modification of the vocalic structure, as in:

Perfect	*Imperfect*	*Imperative*
kataba →	yaktubu →	uktub
nazala→	yanzilu→	inzil
fataḥa →	yaftaḥu →	iftaḥ

The elimination of the first vowel of *katab* is justified by a general constraint (any 4CV sequence is prohibited within a word) and the predictability of the alternation of the second (*a/i,a/u,a/a*) in accordance with the consonantal context, and the syntactic, or the semantic properties of the verb, have been debated at length, in particular the relationship between the presence of the *a* and that of a guttural in its immediate vicinity.

2 Derivation 'with augment' modifies the consonantal pattern of the basic structure, by affixation or doubling, to give an augmented form, from which one can thereafter form an imperfect and an imperative. This modification is correlated with the expression of a grammatical 'meaning' (*maʿnā* II). Hence, for example, in the augmented verbal form *'afʿala*, the adding of the prefix *'a* brings about a modification of the properties of the verb, since the verb *d̲ahaba* ('he has departed') acquires transitivity through this prefix: *'ad̲haba* ('he has caused to depart').

Derived nominal morphology

Participles and their intensive forms, adjectives, nouns of time, place, and instrument, and comparatives are derived from the imperfect with which they have a relationship which is formal (they share the same structure, CVCCVC: *yafʿal*, *mafʿal*, *mafʿil*, *ʾafʿal* . . .) and/or semantic. The explanation of the derivational schema (see Figure 4.1) proposed in Bohas and Guillaume (1984), applied to the intensive adjective *ʾakuwl* ('guzzler'), enables one to have a more precise understanding of these processes.

In the first stage, the root (its phonetic and semantic aspect) combines with the meaning (*maʿnā* II) of the process and forms the *maṣdar*. The addition of the tense (past) is effected in the basic verbal structure FAʿALA. Thence, by derivation without augment the imperfect is obtained, then, by nominal morphology, one obtains the participle FA"ʿIL which expresses 'the being of the subject' (the person who is eating) and its intensive form FAʿUWL. The central idea being that every element in the chain of derivation cumulates the 'grammatical meanings' of those which precede it and adds another one. This is how the relationships which exist between the *binya-s*, basic and derived, which can be found in the language are expressed; certain morphological or syntactic properties of the derived forms being deducible from their antecedents.

From the nominal forms, basic or derived, it is possible to form the plural and the diminutive. These two processes are the subject of particularly intensive study because they are often the source of very complex phonological processes.

In addition, *taṣrīf* comprises a procedure of recognition which makes it possible to link all words in the language to one of the structures defined or produced by morphology. This procedure consists of assigning a pattern (*wazn*) to every word (except particles). The *wazn* is itself written by means of the symbols FʿL and the augments are reproduced as they are. Thus, for a word like *istarǧaʿa* ('to demand the return of something'), this procedure allows us to assign to it the *wazn istafʿala*, the perfect of an augmented verbal form, which is the same as saying that *ista* has been recognized as an augment, *r* as C1 (=F), *ǧ* as C2 (=ʿ) and ʿ as C3 (=L).

PHONOLOGY

Each phonetic form having been assigned to a structure, basic or augmented, it is still necessary to explain the discrepancies which exist between these structures and some of their phonetic realizations: for example, the form *qa"la*[3] [*qāla*] ('he said'). The

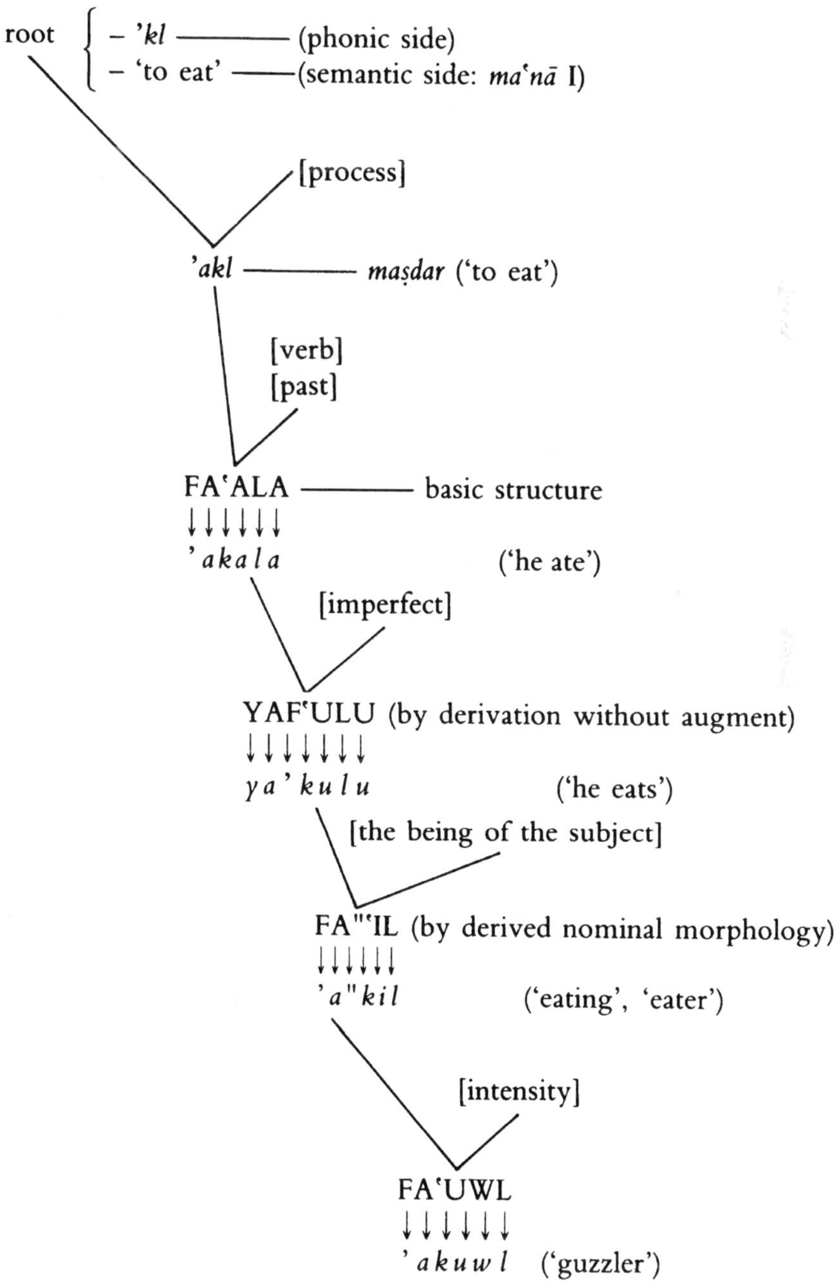

Figure 4.1 The process of word derivation (The various ‘meanings’ (*maʿānī*) are in square brackets.)

procedure of recognition makes it possible to detect the *wazn* *fa'ala*, linking it *ipso facto* to the basic structure FA'ALA ([verb], [perfect]), and permits the identification of its root-segments: QWL. Thus, its phonetic form should be *qawala*. The function of the second part of the *taṣrīf* is precisely to explain this gap between the representation at the end of the application of the identification procedure and the form actually pronounced (*lafẓ*).

This explanation is always conceived in a synchronic system, linking the primary-form *aṣl* to the occurring form, and the relevance of a diachronic explanation is explicitly denied:

> It should be understood that when we say that the primary form (*aṣl*) of *qa"ma* [*qāma*] and *ba"'a* [*bā'a*] is *qawama* and *baya'a*, that of *axa"fa* [*axāfa*] and of *aqa"ma* [*aqāma*] *axwafa* and *aqwama*, that of *ista'a"na* [*ista'āna*] and *istaqa"ma* [*istaqāma*], *ista'wana* and *istaqwama*, that definitely does not mean that we are implying that, at some time, people pronounced *qawama* and *baya'a*, and so on for the forms which undergo transformations, and that this manner of speaking would have been dropped later on. We simply mean that if these forms were pronounced in accordance with the *qiyās*[4] by referring to the forms which are similar to them, the pronunciation would be *qawama*, *baya'a*, *istaqwama* and *ista'wana*.
>
> (Ibn Ǧinnī, *Munṣif*, I: 190)

To illustrate what we have just said about the organization of the *taṣrīf* and the argumentative procedures of AG, we will reproduce the arguments of Ibn Ya'īš about the primary form of the verb *qāla*. This verb, as we have just seen, includes a *w* as second root-segment, but how is it possible to justify referring it to the basic structure FA'ALA rather than to FA'ILA or FA'ULA?

> If anyone should make the following objection: What right have you to say that the verbs of this class, such as *qa"la* [*qāla*], *'a"da* [*'āda*], *ṭa"fa* [*ṭāfa*] and *qa"ma* [*qāma*], have the primary form (*aṣl*) *fa'ala* and not *fa'ila* or *fa'ula*, you shall answer that, in any case, these verbs could not have any other primary form than *fa'ala* (like *ḍaraba* (to strike)), *fa'ila* (like *'alima* (to know)) and *fa'ula* (like *ẓarufa* (to be distinguished)).
>
> It cannot be *fa'ila* because their imperfect is *yaf'ulu*, like

> *yaqwulu* [*yaqūlu*] and *ya'uwdu* [*ya'ūdu*]; the primary representation of these two forms is *yaqwulu* and *ya'wudu*, then the *u* was moved forward. Now we know that *yaf'ulu* cannot correspond to *fa'ila* except in a few exceptional cases, such as *faḍila/yafḍulu* and *mitta/tamuwtu* [*tamūtu*], and an argument can only be based on general facts.
>
> (*Šarḥ al-Mulūkī*: 52)

Granted that the imperfect of *qāla* is *yaqūlu*, which has *yaqwulu* as its subjacent representation, it is impossible to uphold that *qāla* goes back to the basic structure FA'ILA, for the verbs with the basic structure FA'ILA form their imperfect in *yaf'alu*, apart from a few exceptions which do not enter into the argument. Finally, when we are dealing with opaque data, we have no reason to suppose that they are exceptional, but we must attempt to explain them in terms of general and well-established facts.

> It is not possible that it is FA'ULA either, and that for two reasons. The first is that the [ancient] Arabs said: *qultu-hu* (I said it) and *'udtu l-marīḍ* (I visited the sick person), while we know that FA'ULA is never transitive. The second is that if their primary form included a *u* (i.e. FA'ULA) the noun derived from it would be of the form *fa'iyl* [*fa'īl*], as is the case for *ẓarufa* (to be distinguished) and *ẓariyf* [*ẓarīf*] (distinguished), *šarufa* (to be noble) and *šariyf* [*šarīf*] (noble). As such is not the case and, on the contrary, what is said is *qa''il* [*qā'il*] (speaker) and *'a''id* [*'ā'id* (visitor), it can only be *fa'ala* and not *fa'ula*.
>
> (ibid.)

The first argument is particularly clear: all FA'ULA are intransitive; now, the verbs analysed are transitive, therefore they cannot be assigned to FA'ULA. The second brings us back to the chain of derivation on page 77. From all transitive verbs, we can indeed form an active participle, which the AG call *ism al-fā'il*, whereas from an intransitive verb an adjective (*ṣifa mušabbaha*) can be derived which most often has the form *fa'īl*. Since it is an active participle which is derived from *qāla* and not an adjective, it is impossible for its primary form to be FA'ULA.

If, in the course of this argumentation, it has been demonstrated that two of the possible hypotheses must be rejected, then the third must be the right one, that is, the primary form to which the rules of phonology must apply really is *qawala*.

As for the formulation of the rules which describe the passage from the initial representation to the pronounced representation, it naturally includes precise phonetic contexts, but also morphological data which can easily be expressed in the notation FʿL. These rules in their turn are justified by a natural tendency which is supposed to have governed the linguistic behaviour of the ancient Arabs, the only speakers considered to be reliable informants:[5] the lightness (*xiffa*) according to which *a* is lighter than *i*, which is in turn lighter than *u* (*a›i›u*), a gradation which agrees with the sonority scale of modern phoneticians. This gradation distributes all of the segments of the language in the following way:

a i u " y w consonants

⟶

light heavy

Phonological rules are applied in order to avoid 'heavy' sequences, which would have offended the linguistic sensitivity of ancient Arabs, which was characterized by a tendency towards general balance and harmony. As for the phonological processes which make it possible to avoid the manifestation of heavy sequences, they are of several kinds, as described in the following sections.

Substitution (*badal*)

Under this heading come all the phenomena of consonantal assimilation, thus:

> *m* is substituted for *n* when the latter is not followed by a vowel and comes before a *b*, as in *ʿanbar* (amber) and *qanbar* (small), for which the phonetic form is: *ʿambar* and *qambar* . . . If the *n* is followed by a vowel it does not change to *m* and you say, in the plural: *ʿana"bir* [*ʿanābir*] and *qana"bir* [*qanābir*].
>
> (Ibn Ǧinnī, *Mulūkī*: 289)

Sophisticated criteria make it possible to decide which allopone figures in the primary form, examples of which are given in the following subsections.

Morphological parity

One considers all the terms derived from the same root and, if one observes in one segmental position a segment which does not appear in the other terms, one concludes that it has been substituted for the one which appears in the other terms. For example (see al-Astarābā*d*ī, *Šāfiya*, III: 197): *tawağğaha* ('turn one's face towards'), *muwāğaha* ('to face'), *wağīh* ('possessing a beautiful face') and *'uğūh* ('faces'), all derived from *wağh* ('face'). In the F position (first root-segment) there is always a *w*, except in *'uğūh*, where there is a ': we can conclude that the primary segment is thc *w*, that the ' is the substituted segment, and that the primary form of this term is *wuğuwh*.

The lack of peer

It can be seen that substitution has occurred because, if it were not said that the segment in question has been substituted for another, that would imply the existence of a structure which is unknown elsewhere. For example, if we do not say that the *h* of *hara"qa* [*harāqa*] ('to pour') has been substituted for a ', that the *ṭ* of *iṣṭabara* ('to be patient') has been substituted for a *t*, like the first of the two *d*'s in *idda"raka* [*iddāraka*] ('to reach and seize one another'), we are led to suppose the existence of the structures *haf'ala*, *ifṭa'ala*, and *iffa"'ala* which are unknown elsewhere' (al-Astarābā*d*ī, *Šāfiya*, III: 198–9).

The phonetic reasons for the substitution in the case presented above are the following:

> The *n* which is not followed by a vowel is a flexible, weak segment which spreads, due to its resonance, into the nasal cavity. The *b* is a strong plosive segment, and its point of articulation is constituted by the lips. If we suppose that an *n*, not followed by a vowel, is pronounced before a *b*, there is a transition from a weak segment to one that has opposite specifications and which are incompatible with its own, which is 'heavy'. The Arabs therefore put an *m* in the place of the *n*, for the *m* shares with the *n* its nasal resonance and agrees with the *b* in respect of the point of articulation, since it is labial, so that instead of the dissonance existing between the *n* and the *b*, harmony between the sounds is achieved.
>
> (Ibn Ya'īš, *Šarḥ al-Mulūkī*: 289–90)

This requirement for harmony, which constitutes the ultimate reason for the application of the rule of substitution, was a part of the nature of the ancient speakers of the language.

Erasure (*ḥaḏf*)

This process applies particularly to verbs with an initial *w* which, when their perfect is of the FAʿALA class, lose this *w* in the imperfect, for example *waṣala/yaṣilu* ('to arrive'), but keep it in the other cases, for example *waǧiʾa/yawǧaʿu* ('to feel a pain') and *wafura/yawfuru* ('to be abundant'). For the AG, the rule must therefore be formulated in a precise enough way so that it only erases the *w*'s of the first class, but they have also to find an explanation for the fact that it does not apply in a very similar context, that is in the FAʿULA.

Let us pass on to the account of Ibn Ǧinnī:

> When the first radical of a verb the perfect of which is in FAʿALA and the imperfect in *yafʿilu* is a *w*, this *w* is erased because it occurs between a *y* and an *i*, as in *waʿada* (to promise), *wazana* (to weigh), *warada* (to arrive); the forms used in the imperfect are: *yaʿidu*, *yazinu*, *yaridu*, whereas the primary form is: *yawʿidu*, *yawzinu*, *yawridu*. The *w* is erased for the reason we have just mentioned. Our analysis is strengthened by the fact that if the *w* is followed by an *a* it is retained, as in *yuwzanu*, [*yūzanu*], *yuwradu* [*yūradu*] and *yuwʿadu* [*yūʿadu*] and it is based on the word of the Almighty: *lam yalid wa-lam yuwlad [yūlad]* (He has not begotten and was not begotten). Similarly in *yawḥal* and *yawǧal* the *w* is retained because it is followed by *a*.
>
> (Ibn Ǧinnī, in Ibn Yaʿīš, *Šarḥ al-Mulūkī*: 333–4)

The erasure of the *w* is attributed to the heaviness of the sequence in question:

> If the *w* is erased, it is solely because of the heaviness which causes it to occur between a *y* and an *i* in the verb. The *w* is indeed considered heavy and is here surrounded by two elements which are also heavy: the *y* and the *i* [in the primary form: *yawʿidu*]. Furthermore, the verb is, of itself, heavier than the noun, consequently, any additional heaviness which could affect it is felt more strongly than in the

> noun. Since all these elements of heaviness are found together, it is necessary to effect a lightening thereof by erasing one of the elements held to be heavy.
>
> (Ibn Yaʿīš, *Šarḥ al-Mulūkī*: 334)

If the cause of the erasure of the *w* is the heaviness of the sequence *yXwXi*, how can one explain the same fact in the other forms of the verb, for example *naʿidu* (1pl.) (primary form: *nawʿidu*) where this sequence is not met? The AG have recourse here, as in many other arguments, to the principle of class unity:

> They have related all the other forms of the imperfect to *yaʿidu* and said: *taʿidu*, *naʿidu*, *'aʿidu*. They have erased the *w* in these forms, although it was not situated between a *w* and an *i*, so that there would be no difference in the form of the imperfect and that there would be a unique pattern in the imperfect, in addition to the lightening brought about by erasing the *w*.
>
> (Ibn Yaʿīš, *Šarḥ al-Mulūkī*: 334–5)

But if the cause of dropping the *w* is linked with its constituting a heavy sequence, how is it that in the imperfects of the FAʿULA class, like *waṭu'a/yawṭu'u*, the *w* is retained? Given the heaviness scale, a *yXwXu* sequence should be heavier than a *yXwXi* sequence. This objection has been the subject of long debate. It was made by Ibn Ǧinnī himself to his teacher, Abū Alī, who replied that the stability of the FAʿULA class prevented the rule being applied. Indeed, whereas the verbs in FAʿALA can have an imperfect in YAFʿULU, YAFʿILU, and YAFʿALU, those of the FAʿULA class keep their *u*: they are therefore stable and this stability is opposed to all other changes, in particular to erasure. As for Ibn ʿUṣfūr (*Mumtiʿ*: 428ff.), he argues laboriously to demonstrate that the sequence *yXwXu* would be, in spite of appearances, lighter than the other. The justification for this rule has raised many other objections and was an important point in the controversy between the Baṣra and Kūfa 'schools'; for more details about this point, one should consult Kouloughli (1987a).

Mutation (*qalb*)

This process explains the transformations which affect the glides in accordance with their vowel context; hence:

> *Y* is substituted for *w* when the latter is preceded by *i*, not followed by a vowel and not geminated. This is the case for *miyʿa"d* [*mīʿād*] (promise), *miyza"n* [*mīzān*] (scales), *miyqa"t* [*mīqāt*] (date), *riyḥ* [*rīḥ*] (wind) and *diyma* [*dīma*] (continuous rain). In each of these cases, the *y* arises from the mutation of a *w* preceded by *i* and not followed by a vowel. Their primary forms are: *miwza"n*, *miwʿa"d*, *miwqa"t*, *riwḥ* and *diwma*, because they come from *wazn*, *waʿd*, *rawḥ*, *dawa"m* (forms in which the *w* appears phonetically, since it is not preceded by a vowel).
>
> (Ibn Yaʿīš, *Šarḥ al-Mulūkī*: 242)

It should be remembered that for the AG, there are three glides: the *w*, the *y*, and the ", which correspond respectively to *u*, *i*, and *a*. We will study in detail the argumentation of the AG in respect of the intervocalic glide, for example in forms like *qāla* and *ramā*, the primary forms of which are *qawala* and *ramaya*. Ibn Ǧinnī expresses the process in the following way:

> When the *w* and the *y* are preceded by an *a* and followed by a vowel, they are changed into *alif*, except in a few exceptional cases which reveal the primary form and give clues to its composition, or when there is fear of ambiguity, or when the retaining of the glide as such constitutes a sign.
>
> (in Ibn Yaʿīš, *Šarḥ al-Mulūkī*: 218)
>
> Here are some examples in which the mutation has taken place: *qa"ma* [*qāma*] (to rise) and *ba"ʿa* [*bāʿa*] (to sell). Their primary forms are: *qawama* and *bayaʿa*; also *ṭa"la* [*ṭāla*] (to be long), *xa"fa* [*xāfa*] (to fear) and *ha"ba* [*hāba*] (to fear) of which the primary forms are: *ṭawula*, *xawifa* and *hayiba*; an *alif* has been substituted for the two segments *w* and *y*. The same applies to *ʿaṣan* (rod) and *raḥan* (mill), the primary forms of which are: *ʿaṣawun* and *raḥayun*. The primary forms of *ġaza"* [*ġazā*] (to make a raid) and *rama"* [*ramā*] are *ġazawa* and *ramaya* and the change was carried out for the reason which we have mentioned.
>
> (ibid.: 218–19)

As the examples show, mutation can apply to the *w* and *y* of the second radical in the verbs of each class and to the *w* and the *y* of the third radical in nouns and verbs. It is therefore a process whose field of application is very wide. The phonetic context is therefore very precise:

$$\left\{ \begin{matrix} \text{w} \\ \\ \text{y} \end{matrix} \right\} \rightarrow \text{"} \ /\text{a} \_\text{V}$$

The justification of the rule by recourse to the linguistic feeling of the speakers is provided, for example, by Ibn Ya'īš:

> The cause of the mutation of the *w* and *y* into *alif* (") when they are preceded by *a* and followed by a vowel is that the union of similar sounds was distasteful to them. It is for the same reason that gemination is necessary in *šadda* (to tighten) and *madda* (to extend).
>
> (*Šarḥ al-Mulūkī*: 220)

If, in the primary form of these last two verbs, that is *šadada* and *madada*, one can easily see that the sequence of the two consonants can constitute a union of like sounds, one must wonder where the like sounds are in the primary forms *qawala* and *baya'a*. The answer to this question may be found in the *Šarḥ al-Mufaṣṣal* of Ibn Ya'īš:

> It is because the *w* is counted as two *u*'s and the *y* as two *i*'s; as they are both preceded by *a* and followed by a vowel themselves, that amounts to four similar elements . . . . Granted that this is so, they used the *alif* because it cannot be followed by a vowel.
>
> (X: 16)

One can be sure that the sequence of four similar elements will not arise again; indeed, to be unable to be followed by a vowel is, for the AG, one of the distinctive properties of the *alif*.

However, this justification, to which is due the application of the rule, is hardly sound and that is why its field is limited to the ' and the L of words, and that is also why the rule is subject to numerous conditions. The first condition is that the vowel which follows the *w* or the *y* should be supplied by the base and not be of epenthetic origin. The second condition is that 'the application of the mutation process should not give rise to an ambiguous form'; thus in the dual, in *qaḍaya"* for example, the rule is not applied, because its application would give rise to the appearance of *qaḍa"* [*qaḍā*] and the form of the dual would lead to confusion with the singular form. The third condition is that if the word is a noun it should resemble the verbal form; so the rule is not applied to *nazawa"n* and *ǧalaya"n*, for a verbal base in FAʿALA"N does not exist.

If we return to the primary form *qawala* and apply the rule to it, as it has been formulated, we have to ask ourselves another question: if the *w* becomes ", that gives rise to *qa"ala*; now, the spoken form being *qa"la* [*qāla*], how is the disappearance of the *a* effected?

> You should know [replies Ibn Yaʿīš] that mutation applies to the *w* and *y* only after these two segments have been weakened by the erasure of the vowel which follows them. That does not imply that the rule applies to *sawṭ* or *šayx*, for here the glides are not followed by vowels in the base and there is therefore no reason to lighten the sequence by erasing the vowel on the right. If you wanted to change the *w* and the *y* directly into *alif*, in words like *qawama* and *bayaʿa*, when they are still followed by vowels, it would not be possible because the vowel would protect them.
>
> (*Šarḥ al-Mulūkī*: 225)

It is therefore necessary to add all these elements to the formulation of the rule:

$$\begin{array}{l} \phantom{\left\{\begin{matrix} w \\ \\ y \end{matrix}\right\} \rightarrow \text{''} / a \_ \;} \text{V /supplied by the base} \\ \phantom{\left\{\begin{matrix} w \\ \\ y \end{matrix}\right\} \rightarrow \text{''} / a \_ \;} \downarrow \\ \left\{\begin{matrix} w \\ \\ y \end{matrix}\right\} \rightarrow \text{''} / a \_ \; \emptyset \text{ /pattern identical to the verbal patterns} \end{array}$$

The appearance of the forms *qa"la* [*qāla*] and *ba"ʿa* [*bāʿa*] will therefore be explained in the following way:

Primary form (*aṣl*): *qawala* *ramaya*

Analysis: *awa* and *aya* constitute sequences which are rejected by the linguistic intuition of the speakers of the language.

Weakening of the glide by erasing the vowel, which gives:
qawØla *ramayØ*

Changing of the glide to *alif*: *qa"la* *rama"*

As for the *alif*, which is, as we said on page 84, the low homorganic glide of *a*, it is distinguished from the two others (*w* and *y*) by certain properties: it is never followed by vowels; it can never be situated at the beginning of a word; it cannot be pronounced in isolation but must necessarily be realized after an *a*, which is the only vowel after which it can occur; it cannot be geminated; it is not a part of basic structures, either in nouns or in verbs. At any rate, it allows the AG to treat what we call the long vowels in a unified way. For them the *ā* of *qāla*, like the *ū* of *yaqūlu* and the *ī* of *yabīʿu* are composed of two elements: a vowel (*ḥaraka*) and a consonantal segment (*ḥarf*), which allows perfect isomorphy between the sequences CVV and CVC (see Kouloughli 1986).

Transfer (*naql*)

This is a metathesis glide/vowel in certain verbal radicals and in those which present an identical structure: *yaqwulu* → *yaquwlu*. Studying the *naql* will allow us to state precisely once more what the formulation of a phonological process is for the ALT.

> Vocalic transfer is produced in the imperfect of all verbs which include a glide in ʿ position, like *yaquwmu* [*yaqūmu*] (to rise), *yabiyʿu* [*yabīʿu*] (to sell), *yaxa"fu* [*yaxāfu*] (to fear) and *yaha"bu* [*yahābu*] (to fear). Their primary form is: *yaqwumu*, *yabyiʿu*, *yaxwafu* and *yahyabu*; the *u*, the *i* and the *a* have been transferred to the preceding segment. This consists therefore in giving a vowel to a segment which did not have one and taking away a vowel from a segment which had one. In *yaxawfu* and *yahaybu*, the *w* and the *y* change into alif because they were followed by a vowel in the underlying form and are now preceded by *a*. The same applies to the derived verbs with a glide in ʿ position, like *yuqiymu* [*yuqīmu*] (form IV of *qāma*), *yuriydu* [*yurīdu*] (form IV, to want), *yastaʿiynu* [*yastaʿīnu*] (form X, to call for help), *yastariybu* [*yastarību*] (form X, to be sceptical) the primary form of which is *yuqwimu*, *yurwidu*, *yastaʿwinu*, *yastaryibu*. The *i* has been transferred to the preceding segment and the glide is now without a vowel, whereas in the primary form it was followed by an *i*, then the *w* was changed into *y*, by dint of the fact that it is preceded by *i* and not followed by a vowel.
>
> (Ibn Ǧinnī in Ibn Yaʿīš, *Šarḥ al-Mulūkī*: 444–5)

The facts treated here pose a problem both as regards the application of the rules and the justification by having recourse to the linguistic intuition of the ancient speakers of the language. In the simplest cases it seems to be, as we have said before, a phenomenon of metathesis which none of the Arab grammars which are at all consistent has failed to include. As the imperfect of the FAʿALA verb always has the structure yaCCVC, say *yafʿulu* for example, we assume under a *qiyās* that *qawama* has *yaqwumu* for the primary form of the imperfect, and we will have seen that the passage from *yaqwumu* to *yaquwmu* [*yaqūmu*] has been effected by means of metathesis. But why must the sequence *Cwu* be transformed into *Cuw*, when it is commonly found in the language, for example in *dalwun* ('bucket'), and in *ẓabyun* ('gazelle')? Al–Astarābāḏī says expressly (*Šāfiya*, III: 144) that a glide preceded by a consonant and followed by a vowel should not be subject either to transformation or to mutation, for this sequence is light. So does Ibn Yaʿīš: 'When a glide is preceded by a consonant, the vowel does not weigh down on it' (*Šarḥ al–Mulūkī*, 448).

The explanation of the process resembles the one invoked to justify the erasure of the *w* in *nawʿidu*, that is the unity of the paradigm, but here it is broadened:

> The application of phonological processes in these imperfects was made necessary, in spite of the fact that the *w* and the *y* are preceded by a consonant [and are therefore light], by the fact that they have been related to the perfect: *qa"la* [*qāla*], *ba"ʿa* [*bāʿa*], *xa"fa* [*xāfa*] and *ha"ba* [*hāba*]. Since all the verbs constitute one single genus, the speaker found it distasteful that rules would apply to one [the perfect] without being applied to the other [the imperfect].
>
> (Ibn Yaʿīš, *Šarḥ al–Mulūkī*: 446–7)

We therefore have a new case where the application of a rule to a 'light' form is justified by reference to the related 'heavy' form, but this time no longer within a paradigm, but within a 'genus': the verb and its derived forms. The argument is supported by cases where, in order to safeguard the unity of the genus, processes are at work in the forms of the perfect because they are applied to the forms of the imperfect, which are considered to be heavy.

But let us now consider *yaxa"fu* [*yaxāfu*] and *yaha"bu* [*yahābu*].

Ibn Ğinnī says that the *w* and the *y* of their primary form, *yaxwafu* and *yahyabu*, are changed into alif. Now, it is obvious that these primary forms do not answer the phonetic context of the rule of mutation, at least not in the standard conception of the application of a rule, but the latter does not correspond with that of the AG. For them, a rule can always refer to an earlier state of the derivation, and the application of mutation to obtain *yaxa"fu* constitutes an excellent example of this. Mutation, as we have seen, applies in a phonetic context where the glide is preceded by *a* and followed by a vowel. If we consider the primary form *yaxwafu*, we note that the *w* is indeed followed by a vowel and that the context of the right side of the mutation is fully satisfied. The vowel transfer gives the form *yaxawfu* and that is where the context of the left side of the mutation rule is satisfied, since the *w* is preceded by a vowel, precisely the *a* which has just been transferred. This can be set out in the following way:

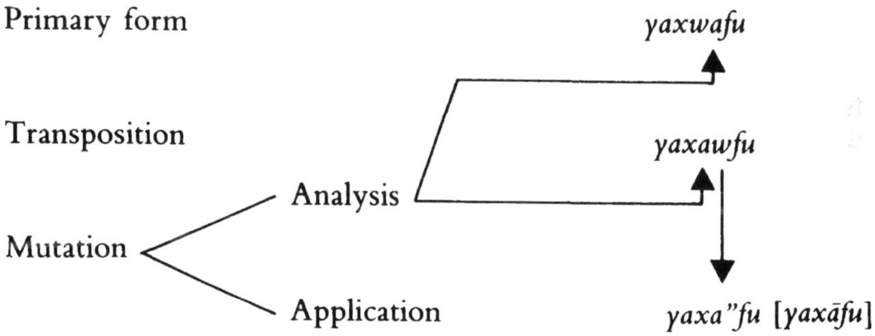

But what will happen in a case where the subjacent form does not contain a vowel, as in form IV of *qāma*, *aqāma*? The primary form being *aqwama*, the *w* is not preceded by a vowel and yet mutation has been applied after the transfer, to give *aqa"ma* [*aqāma*]. This does not create a bigger problem than the *w* in *naʿidu* or the transfer of the *u* in *yaqwulu*: 'If forms like *ara"da* [*arāda*] and *aqa"ma* [*aqāma*] have been affected by changes, it is because they have been related to the simple form' (Ibn Yaʿīš, *Šarḥ al-Mulūkī*: 449), that is *qawama* and *rawada*, where the heavy sequence effectively exists. We see how far the unity of the genus must be extended to justify the application of the rules here.

Gemination (*idġām*)

When the ʿ and the L are identical consonants, two rules apply: a rule of erasure, when the sequence in question is preceded by a vowel, as in *madada*, which becomes *madda*; and a rule of metathesis when it is not: *yamdudu* becomes *yamuddu*.

> In each verb whose second and third root-segments have the same point of articulation, gemination is effected without exception in the perfect, as in *šadda* (to tighten), *madda* (to pull), *ḍanna* (to keep back) and *ḥabbaḏa zaydun* (how handsome Zayd is!). Their primary forms are respectively: *šadada, madada, ḍanina* and *ḥabuba*. The union of such segments, both followed by a vowel, was considered heavy, so that the first consonant was geminated with the second . . . . In the imperfect, the transfer of the vowel is effected, as in *yašuddu, yamuddu, yaḍannu, yastaʿiddu* and *yaṭma'innu*. The vowel was transferred and then the first of the two identical consonants was geminated with the second.
>
> (Ibn Ǧinnī, in Ibn Yaʿīš, *Šarḥ al-Mulūkī*: 450–1)

The phonetic context and the changes effected by the rule are clear, but what is their justification?

> They found it distasteful to unite identical segments, for it seemed to them that it was heavy to move the tongue from a place only to put it back there immediately afterward, which is an irksome operation for it. Al-Xalīl compared this to the gait of a man in chains: he raises his foot and puts it down in the same place, or almost, because his shackles prevent him from moving forward and lengthening his step . . . . When the two identical consonants are separated neither by a vowel nor by a pause, they become, due to the fact that they are so strongly linked, as if they are fitted one into the other, in such a way that the tongue articulates them at the same time, strongly: they found that lighter than to have to raise the tongue twice.
>
> (Ibn Yaʿīš, *Šarḥ al-Mulūkī*: 451–2)

Gemination is not effected, however, in the nouns. It is not, furthermore, the only phonological process which distinguishes the verb from the nouns, applying to the former and not to the latter. The nouns being considered as lighter, the heaviness which is constituted by the succession of identical elements appeared tolerable and did not cause any change.

Gemination having been effected, both elements have a special status:

> 'They are as if imbricated in one another', and 'the tongue articulates them together', and furthermore, they escape certain phonological processes, for example, mutation. It has in fact been established that the sequence *uy* changes to *uw*, as in *muysirun* which is realized as *muwsirun* [*mūsirun*] (easy), but if the *y* is geminated, as in *'uyyal* (poor) and *suyyal* (plural of *sā'il*: liquid), mutation does not take place: if the *w* and the *y* are geminated, they reinforce one another and escape mutation because their status of a glide vanishes, and their resemblance to the *alif*, which is never geminated, is diminished; the two geminated segments have, in fact, the status of a single element, the tongue articulates them together, so that the geminated group has the same status as a consonant followed by a vowel.
>
> (Ibn Ya'īš, *Šarḥ al-Mulūkī*: 497)

The late phonological processes

Finally, *taṣrīf* entails late processes of erasure and epenthesis which are intended to explain the phenomena of pause and sandhi. In both cases, the aim is once more to avoid 'heavy' sequences considered to be 'unpronounceable', which would consist of two consecutive consonants not followed by a vowel. This 'lightening' is effected by erasure or epenthesis.

Erasure

'The erasure of the *alif* occurs in *lam yaxaf* and *lam yahab*. Their subjacent forms are *yaxa"fu* and *yaha"bu*' (Ibn Ya'īš, *Šarḥ al-Mufaṣṣal*, IX: 122). The first stages are therefore known; they bring transposition and mutation into play:

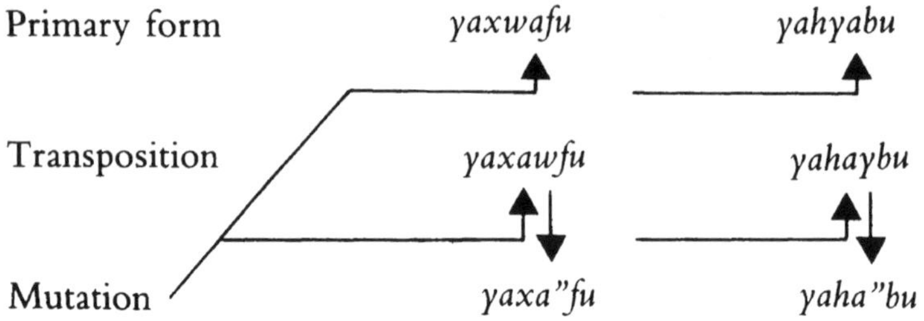

'The introduction of the particle of apocope has led to the erasure of the last vowel. The erasure of this last vowel gives rise to the forms *yaxa"f* and *yaha"b*' (*Šarḥ al-Mufaṣṣal*, ibid.). These forms include a sequence of two consonants without vowels, the " and the *f* or *b*, 'and the " is erased, because of the coming together of the two consonants without a vowel' (*Šarḥ al-Mufaṣṣal*, ibid.). This gives rise to the two attested forms: *yaxaf* and *yahab*. In the forms *yabiʿ* and *yaqum*, it is the *y* and *w* which are erased (from *yabiyʿu* → *yabiyʿ* and *yaquwmu* → *yaquwm*) in a like manner.

Epenthesis

The groups of three consonants are separated by a rule of epenthesis which inserts an *i* after the first one:

> The general rule, in all cases where two consonants without a vowel come together is to insert an *i* after the first, as in *baġat i l-'ama* (the slave fornicated) and in *qa"mat i l- ǧa"riya* (the servant arose), and is not applied only when there is a good reason for not doing so.
>
> (Ibn Yaʿīš, *Šarḥ al-Mufaṣṣal*, IX: 127)

The heavy sequence constituted by *t l '* and *t l ǧ*, which was offensive to the ancient speakers' linguistic feeling, was thus lightened. This heaviness of the three vowelless consonants is presented by Ibn Ǧinnī (*Xaṣā'is*, I: 90) as an articulatory constraint which is a part of human nature and applies 'as well to the black-skinned as to the red-skinned'; but, Ibn Ǧinnī wonders, how then can we explain how the sequence in question is found in Persian, as in *ma"st* ('milk')? For Ibn Ǧinnī that only occurs when the first is an *alif* and, as the *alif* resembles an *a*, it is as if it were *mast*, and two vowelless consonants are permissible in the pausal forms (al-Astarābāḏī, *Šāfiya*, II: 210). Others did not fail to point out that it is not only with the *alif* that the occurrence of three consonants can be observed in Persian, since there are words like *kuwšt* ('meat'). It must be noted in conclusion that it is only in this debate about the coming together of vowelless consonants that any Arab grammarians took any interest, and that only marginally, in the phonetic facts presented by neighbouring languages; for them there was never any question of doing general or comparative linguistics.

PHONETICS

Unlike morpho-phonology, which has remained the exclusive domain of grammarians, phonetics has interested numerous categories of scholars in the Arabo-Islamic cultural system, and has benefitted to various degrees from different approaches. Among these was, of course, that of the grammarians proper, but also that of the specialists of *tağwīd*, the ritual recitation of the Qur'ān, and that of the physiologists. We will try in the following subsections to give a synthetic idea of the most significant contributions of these three approaches to the study of the sound system of Arabic.

The phonetics of the grammarians

It is reasonable to consider that the earliest analysts of the sound system of Arabic were the obscure precursors who adapted the North-Western Semitic writing system to the needs of their South-Western Semitic language. Unfortunately nothing is known about them. Not much is known either about their successors, who, under the impulse of the Umayyad caliph ʿAbd al-Malik Ibn Marwān (d. 86/705) and, according to numerous traditions, under the supervision of the governor of Iraq, al-Ḥağğāğ Ibn Yūsuf, made the Arabic script better adapted to the needs of an administrative language by providing it with diacritic dots and vocalization marks. It seems obvious that the high degree of functional adaptation of the writing system they evolved arises from a profound technical analysis of the workings of the phonetic system of Arabic. But they have left us no trace of their thoughts on that matter.

The first name which may be cited in the phonetic study of Arabic is that of al-Xalīl (d. around 175/791). Various more or less legendary traditions associate his name with the 'invention' of many 'Arabic sciences' such as metrics, lexicology, music, and even mathematics. As far as phonetics is concerned, the fact is that an apparently early lexicographical work attributed to him, the *Kitāb al-ʿAyn*, is arranged according to a definitely phonetic pattern. The lexical units are arranged following a phonetic scheme, that is in such a way that their radical consonants start from the lower points of articulation, in the throat, and proceed upwards to the lips. This explains the title of the book, which is the name of the voiced fricative pharyngeal in Arabic, one of the lowest-articulated consonants in the language. Apart from the direct contributions of al-Xalīl, it should be noted that in many passages of Sībawayhi's *Kitāb* where phonetic and phonological questions are raised, reference is explicitly made to the teachings of al-Xalīl, which suggests that in these matters he may have been considered an authority in his time.

Coming to Sībawayhi, it may be said that phonetics is probably the domain in which his teachings have been most widely and faithfully accepted. In fact, his treatment of phonetic matters is quite marginal, as it comes only at the end of the *Kitāb*, when he discusses the problems of assimilation (*idǧām*) in certain classes of words. Only at that point does he feel the need to give a general view of the classification of Arabic speech sounds, their social classification into high and low variants and the major phonetic traits according to which they are to be classified. His whole presentation of these general questions does not take more than a few pages, but the method and terminology he uses to do so will be re-used with great faithfulness by all his successors, and it may be said that nothing radically new has been added to his basic approach since then.

The classification of Arabic consonants, elaborated by Sībawayhi and practically re-used without modifications by subsequent grammarians, rests on what has to be recognized as a system of phonetic features. These features describe not only the points and manner of articulation of each segment, but also a number of general properties, partly articulatory and partly auditory, which are supposed to organize all the segments into families of sounds. These features generally present a positive and a negative value. Among the most general ones are the opposition between 'loud' and 'murmured' consonants (*maǧhūra/mahmūsa*), which has been the object of much controversy in contemporary linguistic and orientalistic circles, and the opposition between 'strong' and 'soft' consonants (*šadīda/rixwa*).

Sībawayhi's phonetic analysis also clearly differentiates between primary articulation, which gives a sound its basic identity, and secondary articulations, which help differentiate segments belonging, so to say, to the same family. For example 'emphasis' (*iṭbāq*) is clearly identified as a secondary phonetic feature, for the author of the *Kitāb* writes, concerning the so-called 'emphatic' consonants of Arabic:

> As to these four [consonants], they have two points of articulation with the tongue . . . and were it not for emphasis [ṭ] would become [d], [ṣ] would become [s] and [ẓ] would become [d̠]; as to [ḍ] it would no longer exist in the language for there is no other sound sharing the same point of articulation.
>
> (*Kitāb*, II: 406)

The problematic status of syllables in Arabic linguistic studies has already been alluded to and will again be touched upon in the chapter on metrics (Chap. 7). It seems appropriate, in this section dealing with the phonetic intuitions of the Arabic grammarians, to mention that the terms for 'consonant' and 'vowel' universally used in the technical literature, that is *ḥarf* and *ḥaraka*, respectively mean, as far as etymology is concerned, 'limit' and 'movement'. This suggested to some scholars (particularly Hadj-Salah 1971) that there might very well be, hidden behind these acccepted terms, an intuition, if not an explicit theory of syllable structure. This idea is further strengthened by the fact that the simplest syllabic sequence, that formed by a consonant followed by a vowel, received in the Arabic linguistic tradition the name of 'mobile segment' (*ḥarf mutaḥarrik*), while the final consonant of a closed syllable was qualified as 'quiescent' (*sākin*). If this admittedly does not constitute a fully-fledged syllabic theory, it would, however, be a very weak position indeed to maintain that this consistently 'kinetic' terminology does not suggest a coherent conception of the dynamic aspects of consonant–vowel combination and that it is only an inexplicable and non-significant metaphor.

The precision and sophistication of Arabic phonetic scholarship has led some orientalists to hypothesize an Indian influence on the elaboration of these ideas. But as far as we know, no convincing argument has ever been proposed in support of this view.

The next great name in Arabic phonetics after Sībawayhi is Ibn Ǧinnī (d. 392/1002). He is the author of the first book almost exclusively devoted to the study of the phonetic properties of Arabic,' a book which he entitled *Sirr ṣināʿat al-iʿrāb*. His other well-known book, 'The Peculiarities' (*Xaṣā'iṣ*), also abounds in phonetic observations. Ibn Ǧinnī seems to have been the first grammarian to clearly and unambiguously recognize vowels as phonetic segments on a par with consonants though differing from them on account of their manner of articulation. He also seems to have clearly felt the functional complementarity between these two major classes of sounds with respect to the constitution of syllables. Some passages of these two texts even suggest that he had perceived the linguistic importance of stress and intonation, a fact which, if properly ascertained, would belie the widely received opinion that Arabic linguists completely failed to recognize these phenomena. Moreover, Ibn Ǧinnī proposed a detailed analysis of the phonotactic constraints which bear upon the collocational possibilities of consonants in an Arabic root.

The phonetics of the reciters

It is generally admitted that the first way in which the Qur'ān was learnt and transmitted was through oral tradition. Actually, even after the establishment of the ʿU̱tmānian corpus, this mode of transmission remained the main one. The best witness to this is that the Islamic community had to admit that there existed seven more or less divergent oral traditions (*qirā'āt*) concerning the rendering of a number of passages in the sacred text. These recognized oral traditions were the object of careful codification, and more generally, the ritual recitation of the Qur'ān evolved quite early into a fully-fledged technical specialization requiring long and painstaking training.

There exists an abundant literature on the art of ritual recitation (*taǧwīd*) but it should be borne in mind that a great number of the technical terms used to describe the modes of articulation of sounds, the proper rhythm, and the techniques of pausing cannot be properly understood without empirical demonstrations from specialists who have mastered the art of recitation through practice with experienced masters.

On the whole, the field of *taǧwīd* constitutes an invaluable source of information on a number of questions relating to the phonetics of Arabic. This is essentially due to the fact that it was essential to this mainly empirical discipline to record in extremely fine detail the phonetic realization of every sound of the Arabic language and to keep track of the minutiae of the modification of the articulatory and/or acoustic properties of each sound in almost every possible environment.

One of the domains in which a careful study of the techniques of *taǧwīd* could be most rewarding is doubtless that of the prosodic properties of Arabic. In many instances, it is crucial that certain pauses be respected or, on the contrary, forbidden in the recitation of the Qur'ān lest the meaning should be gravely impaired. Consequently, the specialists of *taǧwīd* developed an impressive descriptive apparatus indicating to the reader when to observe an obligatory pause, or a facultative one, and when continuous reading is mandatory.

This information is all the more important because it still has a physical realization through the techniques of recitation transmitted from generation to generation to the specialists of *taǧwīd*. Unfortunately, too little scholarly work has been conducted in this field so that most of what could be learnt from it still remains to be discovered and interpreted.

The phonetics of the physiologists

What we have in mind in this last section is essentially the research conducted by physicians on the workings of the human vocal apparatus. The work most representative of this research is undoubtedly Ibn Sīnā's (d. 429/1037) book on 'The Causes of the Production of Speech Sounds' (*Asbāb ḥudūṯ al-ḥurūf*). It is a very brief treatise presenting in no more than a score of pages almost all that was known to Arabic physiology about the production of speech sounds. The book is divided into six chapters respectively devoted to the following issues:

the cause of the production of sound (in general);
the cause of the production of speech sounds;
the anatomy of the vocal apparatus;
the analysis of each Arabic speech sound;
the analysis of non-Arabic speech sounds;
the non-vocal synthesis of speech-like sounds.

Among the things that one is surprised to discover, when

reading this booklet, is the fact that the vibratory nature of sound and the basic structure of the auditory process had been correctly identified. This is what Ibn Sīnā writes on the subject:

> I think that the immediate cause of sound is the strong and fast undulation (*tamawwuǧ*) of the air whatever the cause of this may be . . . Then that wave (*mawǧ*) is transmitted to the still air in the auditory meatus and makes it vibrate (*yumawwiǧuhu*) so that the nerve spread over its surface can feel that.
>
> (*Asbāb*: 4–5)

This text may also be the first one, as far as we can tell, that correctly identifies the role of the larynx and the vocal cords in the production of speech sounds. In his third chapter, Ibn Sīnā, after giving a detailed description of the different components of the laryngeal cavity and their movements relative to one another, says that these movements cause a narrowing or a widening of the pharynx and that this is the reason for the acute or grave quality of sounds.

Finally, this treatise may very well be the first one to have tackled the question of the artificial synthesis of speechlike sounds. In the last chapter a number of experimental ways of producing sounds imitating those produced by human beings are suggested, and conclusions are drawn from these experiments concerning the way speech-sounds are actually produced by humans.

NOTES

1 In the field of *taṣrīf*, *ma'nā* has two meanings:

> the semantic content of a root, e.g. the concept 'strike' linked to *ḌRB*;
> the syntactico-semantic properties of a form.

We will therefore speak of *ma'nā* I and *ma'nā* II when we want to refer precisely to each of them.

2 The syntactico-semantic properties *ma'nā* II of each of these forms are the following:

> *ḍaraba*: [verb], [past]
> *ḍarraba*: [intensivity], [verb], [past]
> *taḍarraba*: [middle voice] of *ḍarraba*
> *taḍāraba*: [middle voice] of *ḍāraba*
> *'iḍṭaraba*: [middle voice] of *ḍaraba*.

3 For the ALT, all long vowels are analysed into a vowel followed by a

homorganic glide which constitutes the element which prolongs the vowel. There are three glides: *w*, homorganic with *u*; *y*, homorganic with *i*; and the alif, which we symbolize with ", homorganic with *a*. In order to facilitate reading, we also give the usual transcription in square brackets.

4 See pp. 22–6.

5 See pp. 26–30.

5

MAJOR TRENDS IN THE STUDY OF TEXTS

Besides grammar, whose historical development and logical structure have been presented in the previous chapters, Arabic culture evolved interesting approaches to the analysis of language and texts in four other fields of research: literary criticism (*naqd*), rhetoric in the Greek sense (*xaṭāba*), the foundations of jurisprudence (*uṣūl al-fiqh*), and rhetoric in the Arabo-Islamic sense (*balāğa*). The common denominator of these four fields of research is that they are all concerned, though for different reasons, with the study of texts, whether literary, religious, or legal. That is why the present chapter will be devoted to a brief presentation of them. One should not forget, however, that although these four disciplines were considered different both from grammar and from each other, they all belonged to the same cultural fabric, so that quite often one and the same scholar could be involved in the practice of two of them or even more. Consequently, it should not be surprising to see that many questions were the object of discussion in more than one of these fields, and that a number of concepts were in use in different disciplines, sometimes with different terminology.

LITERARY CRITICISM

This field is the more specifically Arabian in scope and method, and is almost entirely concerned with the analysis of poetry. Its first manifestations may be traced back to the pre-Islamic period when, as tradition has it, some authorities were called upon to judge the comparative poetic skills of two or more poets, each claiming to be the best. The reports transmitted to us by tradition as to the content of these judgements suggest that they were based on very heterogeneous views, mingling formal considerations relating to the well-formedness of verse, and semantic ones having to do with what vocabulary was considered appropriate for the treatment of a given theme. Sometimes even moral principles might be called to bear on the overall aesthetic evaluation of poetry. The language used to express these judgements, mostly made up of coarse comparisons and crude metaphors, sounds strangely primitive and wild to the modern reader, and is, at any rate, so subjective that it can hardly be transposed to any situation other than that which gave birth to it. Yet, however archaic and unsophisticated they may be, these views suggest that there already existed, in the Ǧāhiliyya, some sense of the fact that a text could be more highly praised than another for form and/or meaning.

As a matter of fact, it is not before the establishment of the Abbassid caliphate and the evolution of Islamic society from the status of loosely federated Beduin tribes or small villages and towns to that of a centralized empire with important cities and a powerful administrative class, that one finds texts which can really be ascribed to the birth of a critical attitude towards literary production.

Al-Aṣmaʿī (d. 216/831) seems to have been the first author to have composed a study (actually a booklet) on 'Major Poets' (*Fuḥūlat*). But his contribution remained essentially eclectic and subjective and he is remembered primarily as an immense transmitter (*rāwiya*) of traditional poetry and a reference (*t̲iqa*) for all that has to do with the ancient Arabian literary heritage. Al-Ǧumaḥī (d. 232/846) with his 'Classes of Poets' (*Ṭabaqāt*) constitutes the first philological approach to literary texts in Arabic culture. He attempted a historical and geographical classification of poets, both pre-Islamic and Islamic, and attached considerable importance to the question of the authenticity of authorship. This preoccupation was quite new at that time and as a matter of fact ran counter to the widespread habit, very frequent in oral cultures, of ascribing texts to great poets without much worrying about the validity of such ascriptions. Al-Ǧumaḥī's concern with authenticity had probably much to do with the strategic status that old Arabian poetry had gained in the cultural fabric of Islamdom as a key to the lexical and grammatical elucidation of Qur'ān and Ḥadīt̲ texts. But whatever his reasons were, al-Ǧumaḥī may be considered one of the first modern philologists as far as the question of the recension of literary texts is concerned.

On the other hand, and although al-Ǧumaḥī still makes use of al-Aṣmaʿī's primitive concept of *fuḥūla* (literally 'maleness') to characterize great poets, he can be credited with a number of new ideas which would help develop the technical analysis of literary texts in later times. For instance, he is the first author to have established the technical term for literary criticism (*naqd*), a term borrowed from the field of money changers and originally applied to the operation of testing coins to assess their real value. He also contributed interesting views in what one could call an incipient sociology of literature by trying to elucidate such questions as where and why poetry emerges in a community, and how it is transmitted.

With al-Ǧumaḥī the era of precursors in literary criticism came to an end. The age of mature elaboration of this field as an independent domain of scholarship now opened up. This process took place in an atmosphere of lively debate concerning the place of the old Arabic literary heritage and its cultural relevance in the new Islamic community. With the conquests, the Arabs had inherited the economic and cultural achievements of more highly civilized groups, whose elites now fought for their cultural legacy to find a dominant place in the emerging society. This meant objecting to the dominant role that traditional Arabic culture was trying to maintain for itself and led to almost systematic disparagement of everything felt to be typically Arabian. And since the main cultural heritage of the Arabs was, besides the unassailable religious texts, their poetic corpus, it was against that corpus that the most systematic attacks were conducted. One of the arguments of the *šuʿūbiyya* (i.e. the non-Arab elite) was that a dominant role for old Arabic poetry could not be justified in the name of Islam, which had condemned it as basically pagan and impious. It was usually added that this literature could not compare with that of more civilized people as to good taste, nor in matters of edification or entertainment.

Now, considering the fundamental place that old Arabic poetry occupied in the elucidation of religious and legal texts, these attacks were bound to appear to the religious-minded people as potentially jeopardizing the very basis of the new community. It was therefore quite natural that a strong anti-*šuʿūbiyya* tide, defending Arabism and the Arabic literary heritage, should spring up. Two great characters will, in the course of this rehabilitation of the Arab component in the cultural fabric of the new society, make major contributions to the field of literary criticism: al-Ǧāḥiẓ (d. 254/868) and Ibn Qutayba (d. 276/889).

Al-Ǧāḥiẓ, one of the greatest prose writers in the Arabic language in view of the quantity and the quality of his literary production, seized all possible opportunities to display the eminence of the Arabic heritage and to show that there is no field of learning and wisdom in which the Arabs did not make valuable contributions. His epoch-making 'Book of Expression and Exposition' (*Bayān wa-l-tabyīn*) is nothing less than an encyclopaedia of all contemporary knowledge concerning the evaluation of texts and more generally human expression, Arabic or other. It is not an exaggeration to say that everything that has been done in the several fields of text linguistics in Arabic culture since then somehow echoes questions first raised by al-Ǧāḥiẓ in that book. Suffice it to say that one will find within its pages the elaboration of the basic issue which will dominate and direct all important subsequent studies in the field, that of the relationship between form (*lafẓ*) and meaning (*maʿnā*).

With Ibn Qutayba a new step is taken towards the elaboration of literary criticism as an autonomous field of scholarship. His 'Book of Poetry and Poets' (*Šiʿr wa-l-šuʿarāʾ*) contains the first attempt at a structured analysis of the great ode (*qaṣīda*) which constitutes the canon of traditional Arabic poetry. He also sketches in that book what could be termed a pragmatic approach to the major themes (*maʿānī*) found in Classical Arabic poetry by relating these themes to both the intentions of the poet and the expectations of his audience. The thematic approach to poetry was already familiar to the Arabs, but Ibn Qutayba gave it psychological foundations, from which later studies would seldom depart. Most of the other themes elaborated in Ibn Qutayba's book, such as the evaluation of poems as to content and as to form, the question of originality and the notion of plagiarism (*sariqa*) in poetry, or the classification of poets into hierarchical ranks, would remain standard topics in all subsequent studies dealing with the subject. It should be mentioned that this strong defender of traditional Arabic poetry clearly recognized that age is by no means a criterion of literary quality and that modern poets, provided they had a good command of their art, could be just as good as the venerable ancestors. In another famous work, 'The

Secretary's Culture' (*Adab al-kātib*), Ibn Qutayba presents the first global synthesis of the Arabic and Persian ingredients which will form the basis of the new literary culture and contribute to the fixing of the new linguistic standards which will shape Classical Arabic prose.

After Ibn Qutayba literary criticism emerged as a firmly established field of research and witnessed the publication of many technical studies of great interest. Among its major authors we must mention T̠aʿlab (d. 291/903) and his 'Bases of Poetry' (*Qawāʿid al-šiʿr*) and Ibn al-Muʿtazz (d. 296/908) and his 'Book of Embellishment' (*Badīʿ*). The former presents an attempt at a comprehensive classificatory system for all literary texts using the well-known opposition of base and derivative (*aṣl wa-farʿ*) and taking into account both semantic content and formal techniques of composition. The latter, prompted by the quarrel between the traditionalists and the supporters of new trends in poetry, elaborated the first systematic descriptive apparatus for the analysis of various types of figures and tropes at the root of the aesthetic value of poetic texts. The terminology he introduced in this field has become almost entirely standard. Further scholars made interesting contributions, descriptive or methodological, all aiming at providing the critic with the means to rationally analyse literary texts. Notwithstanding this fact, one can hardly shake off the impression that literary criticism will always retain, in Arabic cultural tradition, a good amount of the subjectivity which it inherited from its early promoters.

'GREEK' RHETORIC (*XAṬĀBA*)

The word *xaṭāba*, which, non-technically, means 'oratory art', was used (sometimes alongside the Arabized *rīṭūrīqā*) by the translators of Aristotle's *Rhetoric* to denote the art dealing with argumentation and the regulation of public speech. Two things should be emphasized from the start concerning the way this discipline was introduced and developed in medieval Arabic culture: first, it was essentially considered as part of the integral corpus of Greek philosophy (*falsafa*), and hence almost exclusively a field of study for philosophers and logicians, rather than for literary critics. Second, the interpretation of its place and status in the system of *falsafa* is noticeably different from the one many specialists think it had in the Greek original. This second point should, as a matter of fact, be made even more general, as not only rhetoric but also poetics is considered by Arabic philosophers as an integral part of Aristotle's logic. This appears clearly from the examination of the corpus of logical studies left by al-Fārābī (d. 336/948) or Avicenna (Ibn Sīnā, d. 429/1037).

The way Arabic philosophers justified the inclusion of rhetoric and poetics in the field of logic, was through the establishment of a global parallelism between the objects and methods of the three disciplines. It seems that this was done by reasoning along the following lines: logic is the discipline that aims at demonstration through syllogism; rhetoric is likewise the discipline that aims at persuasion through enthymeme; as to poetics it aims at assent through mimesis (*muḥākāt*) and representation (*taxyīl*). Two basic assumptions seem to justify this twofold parallelism. The first one is that Aristotle himself, though he only regards as a science the theory of syllogisms, admits that rhetoric is 'a replica of dialectics' as a general theory of argumentation dealing with likely premises. And indeed an enthymeme (*qiyās al-ḍamīr*) is nothing but a weak type of syllogism (*qiyās*). The second one is that, in the opinion of al-Fārābī and his followers, the object of poetry is not merely to imitate what happens in the real world, as the Aristotelian concept of *mimêsis* may suggest, but to do so with a pragmatic objective in mind: that of stirring up in the human soul some kind of passion, positive or negative. Hence the two complementary concepts of *muḥākāt* (imitation) and *taxyīl* (suggestion) found in the poetics of Arabic philosophers. In so far, then, as poetry aims at a practical goal, it can be compared to rhetoric and logic. In fact the three of them seem to stand at different levels on a kind of continuum of techniques dealing with the means of influencing humans through language.

Although the corpus of texts devoted to the 'philosophical' analysis of poetics and rhetoric is by no means negligible, the philosophers made no attempt to apply their theoretical views to the study of actual literary texts, so that their contribution to the field of text linguistics has remained essentially speculative. It has already been mentioned, regarding this point, that Greek conceptions do not seem to have exercised a profound influence on the actual practice of literary criticism in the Arabic-speaking world. There are, however, a number of exceptions to that principle, three of which, at least, deserve mentioning.

The first, and possibly the most influential one is Qudāma

Ibn Ǧaʿfar (d. 337/948). His 'Critique of Poetry' (*Naqd al-šiʿr*) intends to lay the foundations of a science of poetical criticism whose object would be 'to differentiate good poetry from bad'. Qudāma emphasizes that questions having to do with metrics, prosody, rhyme, or lexical choices are not an integral part of such a science but only interfere with it in an accidental, secondary way. Slightly modifying al-Fārābī's conceptions, he defines poetry as 'metricalized rhymed meaningful utterances' and then sets out to analyse its simple elements, form, meaning, meter, and rhyme: for each he tries to find the positive and negative attributes which make it good or bad. He then passes to the complex unities resulting from the various combinations of simple elements (form and meaning, form and meter, meaning and meter, etc.), and likewise seeks to establish their positively and negatively valued attributes. The study of meaning is devoted the largest amount of space. In this respect Qudāma essentially continues the traditional conceptions in that he considers that the meaning of a verse is essentially equivalent to the intentions (*aġrāḍ*) which caused the poet to produce that verse. These intentions boil down to six major types, which of course turn out to constitute a typology of poems: the panegyric (*madīḥ*), the satire (*hiǧā'*), the elegies (*marāṯī*), the comparison (*tašbīh*), the description (*waṣf*), and the love poem (*nasīb*). These 'meanings' can be assessed according to a number of attributes, positive or negative, such as correct (or incorrect) oppositions, or respect (or transgression) of usage.

The basic idea in Qudāma's system is that the assessment of a piece of poetry must proceed from simple to complex units, and for each unit recourse should be had to a precise and finite set of attributes positively or negatively valued. The overall valuation would then emerge as the algebraic sum, as it were, of the partial evaluation procedures applied to the smaller units. This method seems to have strongly appealed to the contemporaries of Qudāma and their successors for its simplicity and methodic aspect. In more or less modified form it has survived in many treatises on poetics. Qudāma's work may also be considered as having established the basic terminology of Arabic literary criticism, and later usage in this field will introduce only minor changes in content or form. The considerable success of Qudāma seems to have been due to the happy synthesis he achieved between the purely Arab tradition of *naqd*, from which he borrowed most of his concepts and aesthetic judgements, and the contributions of *falsafa*, on which the essentials of his method are based.

The second adapter of the Greek approach to literary criticism is a contemporary of Qudāma, Isḥaq Ibn Wahb (fourth/tenth century). His book devoted to these questions was first published in 1932 under the title of 'Critic of Prose' (*Naqd al-naṯr*). This title and the strong Aristotelian flavour of its contents first led some specialists to wrongly attribute it to Qudāma. However, notable discrepancies between the approaches developed in the two books and the very strong Šiʿite bias in Ibn Wahb's text led Ṭaha Ḥusayn to question this attribution, and about sixteen years later another manuscript of the book made it possible to identify the real author and the real title of the work: 'The Demonstration on the Modes of Expression' (*Al-Burhān*). This book can be characterized as both an elaboration on Ǧāḥiẓ's previously mentioned study, and an extensive adaptation of Aristotle's views on poetics and rhetoric. Like Ǧāḥiẓ, Ibn Wahb considers that linguistic expression is but one of several modes of expression available to man, and like him he seems to aim at an encyclopaedic presentation of all of them. And indeed the book touches a large number of issues, including logic (to which the author devotes a good number of pages) and even questions hinging on hermeneutics and jurisprudence. In the specific field of literary criticism Ibn Wahb treats both poetry (which he does not characterize in purely formal terms as Qudāma did) and prose. Concerning this latter field of inquiry, Ibn Wahb, following Aristotle, divides expression into two basic types: assertion (*xabar*) and command (*ṭalab*), the first type being the only one constituting a judgement and hence liable to truth or falseness. This dichotomy was not unknown in the Arabic technical literature on the analysis of texts: it was familiar to Ǧāḥiẓ and Ibn Qutayba, and it played an important classificatory role in Ṯaʿlab's book on poetry. But Ibn Wahb's religious convictions lead him to discuss under this heading very specific problems relating to the Šiʿite practice of *taqiyya*, the lawful right to lie under oppressive governments, or to their theory of *badā'*, God's aptitude to change His mind. An important part of the book is devoted to the analysis of specifically grammatical questions relating to the structure of linguistic expressions in Arabic. Ibn Wahb thus treats problems of morphology, regular and irregular lexical derivation, and other technical points such as word order and the organization of sentences in a text. Ibn Wahb also discusses at length a number of questions which were considered strategic at that time in literary criticism: namely the diverse types of tropes, and figures of composition such as allusion, symbolic expression, exaggeration, understatement, etc.

Ibn Wahb's treatment of poetry is more faithful to Aristotle's approach than Qudāma's. Ibn Wahb follows Aristotle in his characterization of poetry as untruthful and proposes a gross adaptation of the Stagirite's typology of verse to the Arabic context. Apart from this, he harps on the classical string of the need to adapt one's discourse to the situation and the addressee and to give every audience what suits their needs. On the whole, Ibn Wahb's book gives the impression that its author strived to strictly follow Aristotle's approach in his books on rhetoric and poetics. This and the obscurities of the man's style possibly explain why his book has remained rather unknown to the general public for a long time.

The last important follower of the philosophers' teachings in rhetoric and poetics is Ḥāzim al-Qarṭāǧannī (d. 684/1285). In his work 'The Way of Eloquent People' (*Minhāǧ al-bulaġa'*), which appears in a historical and theoretical setting notably different from that of the previous authors, he tries to formulate a global system integrating technical elements from the field of Arabic rhetoric (*balāġa*) into a logical framework essentially based on Greek rhetoric and poetics. Yet he intends to consider this framework in itself, that is independently from the logical and philosophical environment in which it was traditionally set within the system of *falsafa*. But this leads, inevitably, to a considerable reduction of the importance of rhetoric as such, because all its argumentative aspects, which connect it to logic, tend to be more or less neglected. Consequently, poetics appears as the major concern of Ḥāzim and his contribution to this field sounds indeed wider and more profound than those of his predecessors. To begin with, his conception of what poetry is appears obviously different from the purely descriptive, and somehow superficial definition of a Qudāma. Ḥāzim insists on the twin concepts of *muḥākāt* (imitation) and *taxyīl* (suggestion) as constituting the necessary and sufficient ingredients of any poetical discourse. As to the classical question of whether poetical discourse is true or false (a question to which it was usual, following Aristotle, to answer with the second term of the alternative), Ḥāzim retorts that it is completely inessential to poetry. The essence of poetry, he says, is quite indifferent to this opposition, because it does not aim at giving knowledge about things but at creating, through a specific process of representation (*tamṯīl*) of things, an attitude towards them, and this, he says, is something basically alien to things in themselves and hence to truth or falsehood. Ḥāzim al-Qarṭāǧannī's contribution remained rather aloof from the major trends of research in literary criticism. Yet it appears to us as astonishingly modern in its search for an essence of the poetic and in its defence of the autonomy of literary art, far from the temptations of commitment or the lure of didacticism.

THE FOUNDATIONS OF JURISPRUDENCE

'The science of the foundations of jurisprudence' (*ʿilm uṣūl al-fiqh*) has as its object the elaboration of legal rules (*al-aḥkām al-šarʿiyya*) on the basis of legal sources (*al-adilla al-šarʿiyya*). The first systematic contribution in this field was the 'Thesis on the Foundations of Jurisprudence' (*Risāla fī uṣūl al-fiqh*) by al-Šāfiʿī (d. 150/767). Its author established the four legal sources of Islamic jurisdiction as being, by order of importance, the Qur'ān, the *sunna* (received custom) as embodied in *ḥadīṯ* (reports of sayings and/or acts of the Prophet), the agreement of the community (*iǧmāʿ*), and finally analogical reasoning (*qiyās*). This classification was accepted by later *uṣūlī* scholars who developed the discipline, such as Ġazālī (d. 505/1111), whose 'Selection' (*Mustaṣfā*) is one of the major references in the field.

The importance of the *uṣūlī* reflection on language and the study of texts stems from the fact that the first two sources of Islamic jurisdiction, namely the Qur'ān and Ḥadīṯ are textual sources written in a rather archaic form of Arabic and hence needing thorough linguistic investigation if one is to be sure of their proper comprehension. Moreover, it is quite natural that ordinary people should establish legal conventions and contracts among themselves and resort to everyday language for this purpose, so that the *uṣūlī* was also faced with the necessity of studying the ways and rules of ordinary language in order to assess the legal validity of such conventions and contracts. Consequently the specialists of *uṣūl al-fiqh* had, by professional obligation, to deal with linguistic questions relating to the study of texts and to develop a good grasp of the rules governing the use of language, both archaic and contemporary. As a result of this twofold constraint, the *uṣūlī* reflection on language developed in two directions, theoretical and descriptive. In the first direction they elaborated complex theories on the general relationship between linguistic form (*lafẓ*) and meaning (*maʿnā*) and the diverse possible modalities of this relationship. In the second direction they evolved sophisticated models accounting for such specific questions as the meaning of conditional sentences or the scope of determiners, quantifiers, and exceptive particles in Arabic.

We will hereafter try to give the reader a very simplified account of some of the general questions raised in this field of research. It should be borne in mind, while reading it, that all of the topics touched on here have been the object of very long and elaborate discussions loaded with arguments and counter-arguments, and that it would take a whole volume to present them in any detail.

One of the major theoretical issues discussed by the *uṣūlī* scholars was that of the origin of language. Two main theories were elaborated on this subject: the first was that language was originally established by a convention (*iṣṭilāḥ*) men passed among themselves; the second was that it was the result of a decree (*tawqīf*) enacted by the Originator of language (*wāḍiʿ al-luġa*). The followers of the first view argued that it was asserted in the Qur'ān that 'We sent no Prophet unless with the tongue of his people, in order that he enlighten them' (Qur'ān, 14, 4), which meant, according to them, that languages preceded God's sending any decree to His creatures. The opponents of this view retorted that it was unambiguously said in the Holy Book that God 'taught Adam all the names' (Qur'ān, 2, 31) and, more generally, that 'He taught man what he did not know' (Qur'ān, 96, 5). Of course, each party proposed an interpretation of the crucial texts that nullified their opponents' arguments. Oddly enough, the supporters of each theory basically made the same objection to their opponents on purely logical grounds: understanding a divine decree, said the followers of convention, presupposes being possessed of language; passing a convention, objected their opponents, is impossible without previously mastering a means of communication. A third party tried to strike a happy medium between the first two: the initial intuition of language, they said, was inspired by the Lord, possibly to just a handful of wise men, and the rest was slowly established by convention. Needless to say this impure theory was criticized by the supporters of the first two, who endeavoured to demonstrate that it came, basically, to admitting that one or the other extreme position was right.

Now these controversies, however deep they may seem, should not obscure the basic agreement of almost all *uṣūlī* scholars on one essential fact: namely, that they considered the relationship between form and meaning to be purely conventional. This position was generally accepted even by most followers of the decree theory, and only a small minority of thinkers in the Arabo-Islamic culture tried to maintain that there could be found a natural relationship between sound and meaning in language. The primary argument which was put forward to support the former opinion was that a given meaning was referred to by different words not only in different languages but even within the same idiom. As to the feeling of the native speaker that there seems to exist some kind of compelling and almost causal relationship between a given word and its meaning, it was explained by the bond of association (*iqtirān*) established between sound and meaning through learning and continual use.

As has previously been said, the different possible modalities of the relationship between sound and meaning received much attention on the part of *uṣūlī* scholars. One of the first distinctions they were led to recognize in this relationship is the difference, essential in order to correctly interpret legal texts, between proper and figurative meaning. Their definitions in this field are roughly equivalent to those in circulation in other areas of text linguistics. What is original in their conceptions is that they admit that what was primarily the proper meaning of a word may very well become archaic or even forgotten, and that some figurative meaning may come to be the only meaning which occurs to ordinary people when the word in question comes to be used. And since spontaneous occurrence of a given meaning (*tabādur*) is considered as the token of proper meaning, they conclude that in such cases the new meaning has become the proper one and that the old one, even though it be the original meaning, is no longer the proper one. This attention to the evolution of language and their firm sticking to the principle that general usage is to be respected when interpreting texts is one of the most interesting contributions of *ʿilm al-uṣūl* to Arabic linguistic thinking.

Another general distinction established by *uṣūlī* thought in the study of meaning was the distinction between two basic categories of meanings: noun-like meanings (*ma'ānī ismiyya*), which can be the object of independent representations; and particle-like meanings (*ma'ānī ḥarfiyya*), which cannot, because they are, by essence, relational. Nouns are, of course, endowed with the first type of meaning and particles with the second. As to verbs, they are analysed by *uṣūlī* thinkers as composed of a substance (*mādda*) and a form (*hay'a*): the substance of a verb, presented as being its verbal noun (*maṣdar*), is considered not to be different from any noun, and hence has a noun-like meaning. Its form, on the other hand, is not, the *uṣūlīs* argue, reducible to a noun; otherwise it would be possible to do without verbs altogether in language. Consequently the form of verbs carry particle-like meaning, that is some kind of relational meaning.

Coming to the analysis of sentences, *uṣūlī* thinkers consider that it is necessary that we should recognize in them some kind of relational meaning: for example, when we hear a nominal sentence like 'Muḥammad (is) a prophet' we do recognize the noun-like meanings of the two nouns that make up the sentence, but we also understand something more than these two meanings, something not conveyed by either of the two nouns in isolation, but by the very structure of the sentence. This means that the structure of the sentence carries particle-like meaning. Elaborating this analysis further, the *uṣūlīs* argue that the difference between independent sentences and subordinate ones leads to the identification of two subtypes of relational meaning: the first, found in particles and dependent constructions, and which they call 'fusional' (*indimāǧī*); and the second, found only in independent sentences, and which they call 'non-fusional' (*ǧayr indimāǧī*).

Furthermore, *uṣūlī* scholars think that different levels of meaning have to be distinguished to account for the way language is put to use in effective linguistic communication. The first is the level of linguistic meaning (*dalāla luǧawiyya*), that is the meaning which is evoked in the brain of anyone who knows a given language by the mere recognition of linguistic forms pertaining to that language. This meaning, *uṣūlī* scholars insist, may be produced without any intention of communication: for instance, by some physical device, or by a parrot repeating something it has heard, or else by a delirious person unconscious of what he or she is saying. That is why ensuring effective linguistic communication takes more than the mere production of that level of meaning. It is also necessary, in order to really convey meaning, to endow the linguistic form produced with what *uṣūlīs* call 'assentive meaning' (*dalāla taṣdīqiyya*). Assentive meaning is, in turn, analysed into two components: the first is 'the intention of use' (*irāda isti'māliyya*); and the second the 'intention of effectiveness' (*irāda ğiddiyya*). This last component may be lacking when a speaker utters something jokingly or when a linguist uses a sentence for purely metalinguistic purposes. These distinctions may remind the reader of the ones developed by some modern scholars in the field of language philosophy or by some contemporary trends in linguistics dealing with pragmatics or the theories of enunciation.

ARABO-ISLAMIC RHETORIC (*BALĀĠA*)

Arabo-Islamic rhetoric (*balāġa*) developed essentially out of the large political and theological debate which opposed Mu'tazilism and Aš'arism during the ninth and tenth centuries (third/fourth centuries AH). Among the major themes which crystallized this debate was the important problem of the exact nature of the Qur'ān. This problem involved not only the well-known, if somewhat esoteric, question of whether or not the Holy Book was created, but also questions like: 'What is exactly meant by the dogma of the inimitability (*i'ğāz*) of the Qur'ān?' To the first question, Mu'tazilīs answered that the Qur'ān was indeed created. Consequently, they were inclined, quite naturally, to an attitude which consisted in stressing its non-exceptional aspects as a text destined for human beings and hence having a temporal history and being liable to rational linguistic investigation as any other Arabic text. In fact, some Mu'tazilīs, such as Abū Mūsā al-Murdār (d. around 226/840), even disputed the fact that the Qur'ān could in any reasonable sense be said to be inimitable.

One of the first important theses on *i'ğāz* is attributed to al-Naẓẓām (d. around 226/840), one of the great theoreticians of Baṣran Mu'tazilism and, by the way, one of the masters of Ğāḥiẓ, whom we met earlier. His thesis is known as the thesis of 'diversion' (*ṣarfa*) as it consists in saying that the Qur'ān is not inimitable but just 'unimitated', and this because God, although He challenged the Arabs to imitate it, 'diverted' them from the temptation to do so. This thesis would be very strongly criticized. One of the first to reject it was al-Xaṭṭābī (d. 388/998) in his 'Epistle on the Inimitability of the Qur'ān' (*Risāla fī i'ğāz al-Qur'ān*): not only, he said, does the duplicity implied by the very idea of 'diversion' not become the Lord's greatness, but also, if it were the case, there would be no inimitability at all. It would be for purely circumstantial reasons that the Qur'ān would not have been imitated and not because it is intrinsically matchless. Al-Xaṭṭābī also criticizes the thesis, then current, which ascribed inimitability to the informational content of the Qur'ānic text and in particular to its eschatological message, which is beyond the reach of humans. The author of the *Epistle* insists that the Qur'ān is inimitable because of its eloquence (*balāġa*) which manifests itself by the presence in the Holy Text of all the literary styles recognized as worthy of admiration. Such diversity cannot exist in the production of one and the same human author because of the limitations inherent in the capacities of men due to their inevitably partial knowledge of the language and of the principles that command the art of 'pouring meanings in the mould of words'. The celebrated Muʿtazilī grammarian, al-Rummānī (d. 386/996), also tackled the problem of *iʿǧāz* in his 'Remarks on the Inimitability of the Qur'ān' (*Nukat*). His work is not outstandingly original, as he includes in his argumentation almost everything that had been said before on the question. However, one can find in his book relatively thorough developments on the purely linguistic aspect of *iʿǧāz*, particularly with regard to the analysis of figures of speech and to certain aspects of the phonetic properties of the Qur'ānic text such as assonance.

The Ašʿarīs reply with the now classical study of al-Bāqillānī (d. 403/1012), *Iʿǧāz al-Qur'ān*: the thesis of 'diversion', which al-Rummānī still considered a component of *iʿǧāz*, not only has nothing to do with it but would be, if admitted, its pure and simple negation. As to the sapiential content of the Qur'ān, it cannot be considered as an element of *iʿǧāz* either: other books, whether revealed, as the Jewish Thora or the Christian Gospels, or not, as the books of wisdom of Persia or India, do present a comparable content without having ever been considered inimitable. Al-Bāqillānī sees in the Qur'ān three components of *iʿǧāz*. The first is the fact that it gives information about things beyond the access of human beings (*ixbār ʿan al-ġayb*). The second is that it manifests knowledge of past events, relating to the ancient prophets and which corroborates the contents of the other revealed books, Jewish and Christian, but which the Prophet Muhammad, being unable to read or write, could not access through these sources. The last is its eloquence: 'The Qur'ānic text is so marvellously arranged, so astonishingly composed, it goes so far in eloquence that one has to recognize the creatures' impotence in front of it.' In a sense, al-Bāqillānī's contribution does not seem to take us very far, as it comes to saying that the Qur'ān is inimitable because . . . it is inimitable. Yet there is in his text an intensive use of a term which will have an exceptional future: the term *naẓm*, which may be translated by 'organization' or 'arrangement'. This term seems to have first been introduced by Ǧāḥiẓ in the technical literature on the Qur'ān, and probably meant for its first users something between 'style' and 'literary genre'. In this sense of the word the *naẓm* of the Qur'ān would be unique, in that it is neither poetry nor prose. It seems that it is through elaborating on the content of this word that grammatical semantics slowly emerged from the discussions on *i'ǧāz*.

The Mu'tazilīs took back the offensive with the Qāḍī 'Abd al-Ǧabbār (d. 415/1024) who, in his immense theological compendium 'The Dispenser in Matters of Unity and Justice' *(Muġnī)*, dedicates a whole volume to the question of *i'ǧāz*. His study is almost entirely centred on the concept of *naẓm*, to which he endeavours to give a really operative content. He first presents the conclusions to which his master, Abū Hāšim al-Ǧubbā'ī (d. 321/933), arrived concerning the notion, central in such discussions, of *faṣāḥa*, that is 'clearness of expression'. Such a quality cannot, according to him, be attributed to *naẓm*, understood as style or literary genre, for two reasons: on the one hand, no one can be considered as being the owner of a particular *naẓm* in this sense and, on the other hand, because you will always be able to say, comparing two authors using the same *naẓm*, that one of the two has more *faṣāḥa* than the other. This consequently demonstrates that *naẓm*, as understood in the traditional way, has nothing to do with the superiority of one text over another. Through this, Abū Hāšim arrived at a crucial conclusion: namely, that there is nothing to be taken into account, in the assessment of a text, beyond its form (*lafẓ*) and its meaning (*ma'nā*); there is no third term and hence *faṣāḥa* should only bear upon these two notions.

Clearly, then, 'Abd al-Ǧabbār contests al-Bāqillānī's opinion that the inimitability of the Qur'ān could be ascribed to its specific *naẓm* understood as a 'textual type' which it would own exclusively. It is, he argues, in the particular arrangement of form and meaning that the irreducible specificity of any text resides, and nowhere else should its qualities be sought. ʿAbd al-Ǧabbār takes one more step: he stresses, in order to avoid falling back into a trivial conception of *faṣāḥa*, that this quality is not to be looked for in isolated words: 'You must know', he writes, 'that faṣāḥa does not show up in the isolated elements of speech but only appears in it through association in a specific way (*bi-l-ḍamm ʿalā ṭarīqa maxṣūṣa*).' The Qāḍī identifies three modalities of that association: the selection of terms, their case markings, and their positions relative to one another. He clearly indicates that 'there is no fourth part to these three because either you consider the word or its case endings or its position and such considerations are inevitable in every single word and then in all of them when they get associated to one another'.

The circuit is now almost completed: the Ašʿarī grammarian ʿAbd al-Qāhir al-Ǧurǧānī (d. 472/1078) will start right from where the Muʿtazilī theologian ʿAbd al-Ǧabbār arrived, but he will tackle the problem with his specific mastery of the workings of the Arabic language. He will, in his turn, reprove his predecessor for having stuck to general statements when speaking of *naẓm* in words as resulting from their 'association in a specific way' without really treating the subject in full detail. The objective which al-Ǧurǧānī assigns to himself in his epoch-making book 'The Signs of Inimitability' (*Dalā'il*) is to make the whole question of identifying the *naẓm* of a given text, and hence assessing its value, a technical problem of linguistic analysis. His basic discovery holds in the following: *naẓm*, that long-sought essence of text, of any text, from the most down-to-earth to the Inimitable, can be studied in a rational and analytical way. Its atoms are nothing but the set of semantico-grammatical categories which the language puts at the disposal of its users and whose arrangements according to a limited number of patterns produce the infinity of what may be said, trivial or inspired, human or divine. These atoms and their patterns of combination the old grammarians had discovered a long time ago. But their successors reduced that knowledge to dead rules, devoid of meaning. The science of *naẓm*, whose bases al-Ǧurǧānī claims to have established, would revive it through returning to the study of texts (Qur'ān, poetry, prose) and even everyday language. This science will reveal that the treasures of meanings hidden in texts are always analysable into infinitely varied arrangements of elementary 'grammatical meanings' (*maʿānī al-naḥw*).

The whole subsequent evolution of research in this field boils down to two essential facts. On the one hand, the integration of the 'science of *naẓm*' in the already existing cultural edifice of the Arabo-Islamic sciences of language would take place. Not, however, as its author seemed to wish, in the position illegitimately occupied by grammar, but as an auxiliary discipline: one will first learn the traditional rules of grammar, and then, later, study what their semantic import can be. On the other hand, the disciples of al-Ǧurǧānī will undertake a more or less systematic and diversely inspired exploration of the empirical and theoretical field opened up to research by the master. The next chapter will deal with the most linguistically significant results of these developments.

6

RHETORIC AND GRAMMATICAL SEMANTICS

After al-Ǧurǧānī, the next great figure to emerge in the new field of the semantico-grammatical study of texts was the great Muʿtazilī scholar al-Zamaxšarī (d. 539/1143). His bulky commentary of the Qur'ān, entitled 'The Explorer' (*Al-Kaššāf*), which may rightfully be considered as one of the most representative intellectual achievements in Islamic scholarship, may be thought of as a practical application of the approach laid down by al-Ǧurǧānī. His dictionary, called 'The Basis of Rhetoric' (*Asās al-balāġa*), should also be mentioned, at least for a feature which remained unique in the technical literature on the subject: for each entry, the author distinguished between proper and metaphorical uses. This was, of course, consonant with the Muʿtazilī dogma stipulating that such a distinction is essential to the true faith, which refuses to assign human attributes to God and hence interprets as metaphorical phrases which could suggest that.

About a century after al-Zamaxšarī, al-Sakkākī (d. 629/1228) composed an encyclopaedic work, which he called 'The Key to Sciences' (*Miftāḥ al-ʿulūm*) and which covered all the aspects of linguistic science known to the Muslim world: phonology and morphology, grammar, rhetoric, argumentation, and metrics. This work, whose value has been diversely assessed, is indisputably the most important one, after al-Ǧurǧānī's, as far as Arabic rhetoric is concerned. In it this discipline was given a general structure which it has ever since retained. Following al-Zamaxšarī, al-Sakkākī conceived of rhetoric as divided into two complementary fields of research.

The first one, called 'the science of meanings' (*ʿilm al-maʿānī*), was defined as consisting in 'the study of the properties of the structure of utterances in speech and the evaluation thereof, in order to avoid mistakes in the use of language in accordance with the requirements of the situation [of communication]'. In the field so defined would be treated all the questions relating to grammatical semantics and pragmatics.

The second one, called 'the science of expression' (*ʿilm al-bayān*), was characterized as the discipline dealing with how to 'produce the same meaning in different ways with different degrees of clearness'. In this field would be studied all that has to do with figures of speech.

To these two fields of research, al-Sakkākī added an auxiliary discipline, which he called 'the science of embellishment' (*ʿilm al-badīʿ*), to which he assigned the task of studying the techniques used to adorn the form of texts by the use of semantic and/or formal devices.

Unfortunately al-Sakkākī's style was far from having the ample cogency of al-Ǧurǧānī's, and his prose was too terse and concentrated to be easily understood. Consequently his book, and more specifically its rhetorical part, gave rise to a series of commentaries, which aimed at making his teachings more accessible.

The most influential of his commentators was al-Qazwīnī (d. 739/1338), who composed a commentary called 'The Summary' (*Al-Talxīṣ*). Al-Qazwīnī's book was itself the object of many commentaries, including his own book, called 'The Clarification' (*Al-Īḍāḥ*), so that it can rightfully be considered as presenting the standard form of Arabic rhetoric.

The present chapter will be devoted to a survey of the main themes of grammatical semantics as developed, under the name of *ʿilm al-maʿānī*, in the framework sketched by al-Sakkākī and further elaborated by al-Qazwīnī.

THE GENERAL ORGANIZATION OF GRAMMATICAL SEMANTICS

From the works of al-Qazwīnī on, the technical questions studied in treatises on *ʿilm al-maʿānī* have been divided into eight parts. This is how the author of the *Īḍāḥ* himself justifies this division:

The object of *'ilm al-ma'ānī* may be circumscribed in eight chapters: the first one deals with the modes (*aḥwāl*) of 'informative' predication (*xabar*), the second one with the modes of the predicand (*musnad ilayhi*), the third with the modes of the predicate (*musnad*), the fourth with the modes of the verbal complements, the fifth with restriction, the sixth with 'performative' predication (*inšā'*), the seventh with conjunction and disjunction, and the eighth with the volume of expression. This delimitation is due to the fact that an utterance is either informative or performative because either it has an external reference to which it is or is not adequate, or it does not: in the first case it is informative, in the second performative. Moreover, every informative utterance requires a predicative relationship (*isnād*), a predicand (*musnad ilayhi*) and a predicate (*musnad*): the modes of these three are the object of the first three chapters. Furthermore the predicate, if it is a verb or assimilated to it, may have complements: this is the object of the fourth chapter. Then predicative or complement terms may have a restricted or unrestricted scope: that is the object of the fifth chapter. Performative utterances are dealt with in the sixth chapter. And again, when two sentences follow each other they may be either coordinated or not: that is what the seventh chapter studies. Finally, eloquent expression may, regarding the content it conveys, be either verbose or not, and this is the object of the eighth chapter.

(*Īḍāḥ*: 85)

This apparently very systematic organization of the field of research of 'the science of meanings' is not, actually, as coherent as it might seem at first sight. For example, certain matters dealt with in the chapter on the modes of the predicand, such as anteposing, determination, or modification, should strictly speaking be resumed in the chapter on the complements, for they may apply to any noun phrase and not specifically to noun phrases functioning as predicands. It should be noted that al-Ǧurǧānī's approach was quite different, since he focussed on general linguistic operations independently of where in an utterance these operations could show up.

SOME BASIC TENETS

Superficially, it might look as if the rhetorician's point of view on utterances and texts was not basically different from the grammarian's, since both shared such basic concepts as 'predication', 'complements', and so on. But such an opinion can be maintained only by overlooking the fact that rhetoric set up a completely new paradigm of reflection on language and that even the old terms which were imported from grammar took on another content in this new context.

In order to correctly assess this fact, one should first remember that rhetoricians have consistently defined the very object of *ʿilm al-maʿānī* in reference to such pragmatic notions as 'the requirements of the situation' (*muqtaḍā l-ḥāl*) or 'the situations of communication' (*maqāmāt al-kalām*), which are notions basically alien to the way grammarians, at least the late ones, conceived of their object of study. It is very significant, in this respect, that the basic unit of investigation that the rhetoricians chose was not the late grammarians' notion of 'sentence' (*ǧumla*), but the rather antiquated concept of 'utterance' (*kalām*): the latter, unlike the former, cannot be reduced to a mere sequence of words analysed in terms of well-formedness, but, on the contrary, requires that its conditions of production be taken into account.

Moreover, rhetoricians have systematically interpreted the formal and semantic properties of utterances as related to the communicative functions they fulfil in the interaction between speaker (*mutakallim*) and addressee (*muxāṭab*).

A clear example of this attitude may be seen in the dichotomy established in *ʿilm al-maʿānī* between informative and performative utterances. Such a dichotomy is manifestly a pragmatic one, as it rests on the distinction between two basic types of usage of language: one only aiming at transmitting information to the addressee; the other at actually acting on him or her through language.

Another, even clearer example is to be found in the way informative utterances are themselves divided into three basic categories depending on the state of mind of the speaker regarding the attitude of his or her addressee towards the information being transmitted. If the speaker feels that the addressee has no preconceived opinion at all regarding the information he or she wants to convey, he or she will present it in a simple, plain way, and consequently choose an 'initial' type of utterance (*kalām ibtidā'ī*). If, on the other hand, the speaker has the impression that the addressee is to some degree dubious about the information, he or she will present it in a more forcible manner by using corroborative markers (*mu'akkidāt*), and the utterance will then be of the 'requisitive' type (*kalām ṭalabī*). Finally, if the speaker thinks that the addressee is frankly hostile, he or she will face the addressee with a highly strengthened enunciation, that is with an utterance of the 'denial' type (*kalām inkārī*). This classification is further refined by envisaging cases when the speaker anticipates and attributes to the addressee states of mind which the latter has not actually manifested. Obviously, such a fine typology presupposes that the conditions of production of speech are taken into account while analysing an utterance, an attitude which is quite alien to the grammarians' preoccupations.

Linguistic and non-linguistic contexts also play a crucial part in the way rhetoricians approach the relationship between form and meaning in language.

This is particularly apparent in the way they account for the opposition between proper and figurative meanings. Proper meaning, they say, is the one which is understood in the context-free use of a linguistic item; figurative meaning, on the other hand, needs a context, linguistic or not, in order to be understood.

More generally, rhetoricians distinguish between the 'primary meanings' (*ma'ānī awā'il*) of an utterance, which result from its linguistic analysis, and its 'secondary meanings' (*ma'ānī ṯawānī*), which reflect the intentions and objectives of the enunciator and which are sometimes quite far from the linguistic meaning. Of course, understanding those 'secondary' meanings takes much more than merely knowing the rules of grammar: you also need to know a lot about the conditions in which speech was produced, and to have a good grasp of the strategies used by the speaker to convey what he or she really had in mind.

UTTERANCE ANALYSIS

As has previously been said, the basic unit of investigation in rhetoric is the utterance (*kalām*). An utterance, whether simple or complex, contains a predicative structure (*tarkīb isnādī*), which is to be analysed into four basic components:

a predicand (*musnad ilayhi*), which is the term spoken of;
a predicate (*musnad*), which is the term with which something is said about the predicand;
a predication (*isnād*), which is the relationship or judgement (*ḥukm*) established between predicand and predicate;
constraints (singular *qayd*, plural *quyūd*), which serve to determine the extension and/or comprehension of any of the three preceding components in conformity with what the speaker has in mind.

While the first two components are well known to anyone who is familiar with grammar, the last two deserve special attention, because they reveal how radically different Arabic rhetoric is from grammar in its approach to language.

As to *isnād*, it has generally been considered by grammarians as somehow automatically resulting from the mere presence of a predicand and a predicate. This 'conjuring away' of the operation which puts together the two terms of a predicative structure is very revealing of the grammarians' forgetfulness of the process of production of speech, and of their exclusive attention to the results of speech acts rather than to these acts as such. This is of course correlated with forgetting the speaker in the grammarians' analysis of sentences.

Quite opposite is the rhetorician's attitude. This is, for instance, how al-Ǧurǧānī argues about the need to recognize the operation of predication, besides recognizing predicand and predicate:

> Now, if you have recognized that no information can be imagined if not between two things, that which is spoken and that which is spoken about, you also need to recognize that there is a third term after these two, and this is because, just as you cannot figure out there being information if there is not both [something] informing and [something] informed about, in the same way there can be no information until there is an informant (*muxbir*) from whom it stems and from whom it occurs, so that it is attributed to him and he is responsible for it in such a manner that he be considered right if it is true and wrong if it is false. Don't you see that it is well known that there is no affirmation and no negation until there is someone who affirms or denies so that he be their source and so that he be their asserter and the one who imposes or refuses in that matter, and so that he

be, through that, agreeing or disagreeing, right or wrong, just or unjust?

(*Dalāʾil*: 406)

In this text, the speaker, referred to as the 'informer' or 'asserter', is considered as the source of the predicative relationship and as assuming the responsibility of the truth value of the assertion so produced. This way of considering predication as resting on the activity of the speaker is, of course, consonant with what has previously been said about the classification of utterances by the strength of their assertion. The predication is affirmative or negative, strong or neutral according to the speaker's beliefs and to what he or she anticipates of the addressee's attitudes to what he or she wants to tell the addressee.

As to the concept of 'constraints', it appears as a remarkably unifying instrument of analysis of all the possible operations of determination and specification which contribute to making language fit the communicative needs of its users. For rhetoricians, everything that allows the speaker to make his or her meaning more specific is a 'constraint', whether it be the determiners which restrain the extension of nouns, the complements which define the spatial and temporal location of the event associated with the verb or its *terminus ad quem*, or the different ways of describing entities or actions. Even the corroborative markers whose status has been discussed earlier are considered as constraints applying not to the predicand or predicate but to predication itself, as they allow the speaker to modulate the strength of his assertion.

Of course, 'constraining' (*taqyīd*) is considered a recursive operation: a *qayd* such as the direct object of a verb may very well be specified by an adjective, which would then be analysed as a *qayd* in the first *qayd*. In the same trend, nothing prevents a *qayd* from having itself the structure of a predicative relationship: you may very well wish to specify a noun with a whole sentence, as is the case with relatives. But in such a case this predicative relationship is somehow incomplete, because it lacks the predication element: this is because, however complex an utterance may be, recognizing it as a single utterance necessarily means that it has a single meaning and hence results from a single act of predication. When analysing complex utterances, some rhetoricians sometimes qualify the 'main' predicative structure, the one endowed with predication, as being 'the main sentence' (*al-ǧumla al-ra'īsiyya*) and speak of 'secondary sentences' (*ǧumal ġayr ra'īsiyya*) when dealing with those predicative structures which function as 'constraints' in an utterance. But all consistently reserve the term 'utterance' (*kalām*) to that unique whole resulting from the act of predication.

It might be worth while to observe that the rhetorical notion of 'secondary sentence' does not correspond with the grammatical notion of 'sentence filling a functional position' (*ǧumla lahā maḥall min al-iʿrāb*). For example, relative sentences are not considered as sentences 'filling a functional position' in grammar, while, quite obviously, they would be considered as 'secondary sentences' in rhetoric, since they necessarily play a qualifying role of some sort in an utterance. This fact, if correctly considered, would in itself suffice to show how deep the difference of approach is between grammar and rhetoric.

TYPES OF PREDICATIONS

All grammarians recognized two basic types of sentences, verbal and nominal. Some added to these two more types, which they called 'circumstancial' sentences (*ǧumal ẓarfiyya*) and 'conditional' sentences (*ǧumal šarṭiyya*). This classification, which finds its most achieved form in Ibn Hišām's treatise called 'The Dispenser' (*Al-Muġnī*), was based, as has previously been shown, on essentially formal criteria.

Rhetoricians also felt the need for a typology of utterances, but theirs was not merely formal: it endeavoured to establish systematic relationships between formal and semantic properties of utterance types. In their study of the modes of the predicate, rhetoricians distinguish between verbal and nominal predicates. If the speaker chooses a verbal predicate, they say, it is to stress that the predicative relationship has a dynamic, progressive and/or evolutionary aspect. This is basically because verbs entail a meaning of 'renewal' (*taǧaddud*). On the other hand, verbs being time-bound, using them in an utterance means that the state of affairs predicated is anchored in a temporal series. In contrast to this, the speaker's use of a nominal predicate means that he or she disregards in the predication all dynamic or temporal aspects, since nouns are essentially characterized by permanency (*ṯubūt*). The speaker may, moreover, introduce secondary nuances of meaning in his or her basic choice by limiting the range of a nominal predication or extending that of a verbal one through the use of adequate constraints.

Nominal predications are further differentiated depending on the determination of the predicate. When it is not determined, as in 'Zayd (is) rich' (*Zaydun ǧaniyyun*) the predication only realizes an attribution to the predicand of the property designated by the predicate. When the predicate is determined, as in 'Zayd (is) the prince' (*Zaydun al-amīru*), then the predication aims at indicating to the addressee that an entity which is known to him or her is identical with another entity also known. The new information in this case is neither the predicate nor the predicand, but the fact that the former is to be identified with the latter.

Concerning verbal predication, it might be useful to remind the reader that the objects of transitive verbs are analysed as specifying constraints on the predicate. This seems quite natural when you consider the difference between 'Zayd writes novels' and 'Zayd writes poetry': you actually have two different types of writing (and of writers, by the way) by just changing the object of the verb. This approach naturally led rhetoricians to examine the case of transitive verbs being used without any mention of objects. Al-Ǧurǧānī (*Dalā'il*: 118f.) explains that this situation might arise out of two quite different intentions. The first is when an object is in fact intended and when its nature is quite clear 'from the speech situation or the context' (*bi-dalīl al-ḥāl aw mā sabaqa min al-kalām*). The second is when no specific object is intended at all, because it is the absolute realization of the predicate which is pertinent. It is, for example, the case in this verse of the Qur'ān (24,19): 'And God knows and you do not know'.

Rhetoricians also recognized a circumstantial type of predication, characterized by the fact that the predicate is either a prepositional group (*ǧārr wa-maǧrūr*) or a circumstancial (*ẓarf*). They considered that such predications functioned somehow as a condensed type of verbal utterance (*ixtiṣār al-fiʿliyya*).

As for conditional utterances, they were, as might have been expected, treated as complex utterances, where the protasis (*šarṭ*) is a constraint on the predication of the apodosis (*ǧawāb*).

The typology of predication elaborated by rhetoricians allowed them to reach a high degree of sophistication in their analyses of texts. For example in this Qur'ānic verse (2, 8) 'Among the people are some who say we believe (*āmannā*) in God and in the Last Day while they are not believers (*wa-mā hum bi-mu'minīn*)' they interpret the opposition between the two basic types of predicates as stressing the contrast between what 'some people' pretend to be something new, that is their having become believers, and what is actually going on without any change, that is their being unbelievers. As to the preposition [*bi-*] which precedes the nominal predicate, it is interpreted here, after a negation, as a mark of reinforcement which is here to emphasize the negation of these people being believers.

GENERAL OPERATIONS ON NOMINALS

Nominals, whether they are predicands, predicates, or constraints, are liable to three general linguistic operations having different effects on the meaning of utterances. These operations are determination and/or specification (*taqyīd*), elision (*ḥaḏf*), and displacement (*taqdīm wa-ta'xīr*).

As to determination, its conditions and effects on meaning can readily be understood: a nominal is determined either when it is supposed to be known to the addressee, and this is 'referential determination' (*al-ta'rīf al-'ahdī*), or when the speaker does not mean a specific individual but rather the genus, and this is 'generic determination' (*al-ta'rīf al-ǧinsī*). Specification, on the other hand, has a number of modalities and may be indicated, in Arabic, by many different markers: construct state (*iḍāfa*), adjectives, relative sentences, appositions, and so on. In general, specifications are supposed to give the addressee a clearer idea of what the speaker has in mind and to help him or her identify more easily what is referred to. But sometimes they rather indicate the speaker's attitude, laudatory or derogatory, towards what he or she is speaking about, or else they may just aim at reinforcing the expression.

Elision of an essential element such as the predicate or predicand is submitted to a very general constraint, namely that the context or the speech situation make it possible to recover the elided element. As to the reasons that may justify elision, rhetoricians cite a great number of them, one of the most significant being that an utterance is sometimes much more expressive and forceful when a recoverable element is elided than when everything is flatly exposed.

Displacement has been the object of detailed research since al-Ǧurǧānī. Grammarians had already recognized that some elements of the sentence could, in certain conditions, be realized elsewhere than in their canonical places, and they had enumerated where and on what formal conditions such displacements could take place. But, and this constitutes one of al-Ǧurǧānī's most severe reproaches to them, they never worried about identifying what effects these displacements could have on the semantic content of the sentence. Worse than that, they often explicitly suggested that displacement had no effect at all on the meaning of sentences, as, for example, when they said that when the two nominal terms of a predication are determined nouns you may consider whichever you wish as predicand. This, says al-Ǧurǧānī, amounts to disfiguring the language.

In rhetoric, the basic modality of displacement is anteposition (*taqdīm*) and its most general import is emphasis. More precisely, anteposing a term serves to mark that the relationship of which it partakes is explicitly limited to it. In other words, anteposing is a mark of focussing. A classical example of this is to be found in Qur'ān (1, 5): '*Thou* we worship and *Thou* we implore for help', where the anteposition of the object pronouns of the two verbs serves to focus the predications on the referent of these pronouns.

Sometimes, anteposition only serves to give more strength, as is the case in 'poor Zayd!' (*miskīnun Zaydun*) where the nominal predicate has been anteposed to the predicand.

INFORMATIVE PREDICATION

As could be understood from al-Qazwīnī's presentation (see the first section of the present chapter), informative predication is to be found in those utterances which are liable to truth or falsity. This conception, which probably has to do with Aristotle's heritage, was introduced rather early in Arabic linguistic thinking, as one may find a clear reference to it in Ibn Qutayba's introduction to *Adab al-kātib* (see the first section of Chapter 5). In the field of rhetoric proper it gained wide acceptance as a general principle of classification of utterances, but the way in which it had to be understood remained for some time an object of controversy.

The opinion of the majority was that truth in an informative utterance was its corresponding to external reality and that falsity was its lack of correspondence. This strict and simple dichotomy neatly fitted the purely logical division established by Aristotle. But it was rather alien to the dialectic turn of mind of many Arabic-speaking thinkers. It should be observed, regarding this, that the words rendering truth and falsity in Arabic literally mean 'sincerity' (*ṣidq*) and 'lie' (*kaḏib*), which is very significant of the deep pragmatic bias of the Arabs in all that has to do with language.

In this connection, one opinion, attributed to al-Naẓẓām (see p. 113), maintained that truth in an utterance meant that it expressed the speaker's convictions, whether the judgement it contained corresponded to external reality or not. This shift from the logical relationship between language and the external world to the more psychological bond between utterance and conviction is very characteristic of the original Arabic approach to linguistic communication.

An attempt at conciliating the two conflicting approaches is attributed to al-Ǧāḥiẓ. It consists in saying that truth must meet the two requirements of correspondence with reality and expression of the speaker's conviction. This leads the great Muʿtazilī author to conceive of falsity as resulting from the conjunction of non-correspondence with reality and expression of the speaker's conviction. The remaining two possibilities, that is correspondence or non-correspondence combined with the absence of conviction, are characterized by al-Ǧāḥiẓ as non-truth and non-falsity.

Discussing the arguments and counter-arguments presented by the followers of each doctrine could surely throw some light on certain deep mental mechanisms commanding the old Semitic attitude towards language, reality, and truth. But we will not delve into such a discussion here, for it would take us too far afield from the main object of the present chapter.

Coming back to informative utterances, it should be remembered that they were basically supposed to inform the addressee of the existence of a state of affairs which he or she did not know of. This standard use is known as the transmission of 'the content of information' (*fā'idat al-xabar*). Yet, it may happen that an informative utterance is addressed to someone who pertinently knows about its content, such as when you say to a non-amnesic interlocutor: 'You stayed home yesterday.' In such cases you do not intend to inform your addressee of the content of the utterance but of the fact that you know about that content. This the Arab rhetoricians call 'the implication of information' (*lāzim al-fā'ida*). This type of use of informative utterances may be appropriate in some situations of communication, as when you want to make it clear that you are not going to be fooled. In other cases it may be used to reproach the addressee for not doing what he ought to do, as, for example, when you say to someone 'but so-and-so is your brother!', meaning that he or she is not behaving appropriately with his/her brother.

Besides these two basic types of use of informative utterances, some rhetoricians recognized a lot more, and long lists of 'aims' (*aǧrāḍ*) were proposed. But actually these numerous potential values are to be recognized as 'secondary meanings' derived from context and situation and not intrinsic values of the utterances.

PERFORMATIVE PREDICATION

As has previously been said, performative utterances are defined as those utterances which are not liable to truth or falsity. They are called 'performative' (*inšā'*) because their very realization aims at performing an act such as asking a question, giving an order, or instituting a new state of affairs, particularly in legal proceedings.

Performative predication is divided into two basic types by Arab rhetoricians: the first type, which they call 'rogative performative' (*inšā' ṭalabī*), basically serves to express requests; the second type, called 'non-rogative performative' (*inšā ǧayr ṭalabī*) does not basically serve such a purpose.

The main subtypes of rogative performatives are order, prohibition, inquiry, wish, and calling. The main subtypes of non-rogative performatives are 'contractual formulae' (*ṣiyaǧ al-'uqūd*) such as 'I agree' (*qabiltu*) used to express acceptance of a bargain, expressions of astonishment as conveyed by exclamatory forms, oaths, and expressions of praise or blame.

For each of these subtypes rhetoricians would record all its possible linguistic expressions, give a definition of its 'primary meaning', and list all its possible secondary meanings illustrating them with passages taken from the Qur'ān, poetry, literature, and even the daily use of language.

Here is, for example, a condensed presentation of their study of command (*amr*).

Command is basically expressed in Arabic by the imperative, the jussive accompanied by a specialized particle, special invariable forms such as [*hušš!*], which means 'silence!', the verbal noun replacing the imperative, and in some specific cases the imperfect verb, as in the Qur'ān (2, 228) 'divorced women will wait during three menstrual periods', or even the verbless utterance in the power of an imperative.

The 'primary meaning' of command is defined as 'demanding the execution of an action from the superior to the inferior' (there follows a discussion of the inadequacies of rival definitions).

But a number of 'secondary meanings' are recognized for this type of performative utterance, in particular solicitation, wish, the expression of hope, supplication, challenge, permission, threat, and many more.

A general principle is posed by rhetoricians, stipulating that performative and informative sentences are basically incompatible, and consequently should not occur in the same utterance. Yet counterexamples abound in the literature, seemingly contradicting this principle: it is the case, for instance, in the celebrated introductory verse of Abū Nuwās which says 'Desist from blaming me for indeed blame is temptation' (*Daʿ ʿanka lawmī fa-'inna l-lawma 'iġrā'u*), where clearly the first part of the utterance is a rogative performative while the second is a (reinforced) informative form. Such situations, of course, led to elaborate discussions aimed at establishing that an informative sentence may have performative value and vice versa.

THE SCOPE OF PREDICATIONS

Just as nominal terms may be determined or undetermined, the predicative relationship may be presented as being valid in general or as having a restricted scope of validity. Restricting the validity of a predication is an operation of great semantic import and has consequently been studied as a specific chapter of *ʿilm al-maʿānī*.

Rhetoricians identified three basic techniques for restricting the scope of predications in Arabic.

The first one, which we have already touched upon when

discussing anteposition, consists in 'focalizing' a nominal term, that is setting it in initial position in order to indicate that predication is specifically referred to it. Not only the subject and objects (direct or indirect) of a verb may be so anteposed for restriction, but also most other complements.

The second technique consists in coordinating two predications: one positive bearing on the validated term and the other negative, and either bearing on another, explicitly excluded term, or completely general, and hence excluding everything but the term validated in the first predication. An instance of the first type would be something like 'Zayd is intelligent, not ʿAmr', and an instance of the second 'Zayd is intelligent and nobody else'. The second predication may be formally incomplete, the lacking elements being easily recoverable from the context as in 'Zayd is not a doctor but a philosopher.'

The third technique of restriction of the scope of utterances is that of exceptive utterances, as in the Qur'ān (35, 28) 'the only ones to fear God, of His creatures, are those who know'.

Rhetoricians refined their analysis of restriction by further distinguishing the cases when the restricted term (*maqṣūr*) is the qualified one (*mawṣūf*), as in 'Only Zayd is generous', and those when it is the qualifying one (*ṣifa*), as in 'Life is nothing but painful'.

They also distinguished, from the addressee's point of view, between three distinct types of restriction:

> one in which the addressee associated two terms with a predication, and the restriction excludes one of them;
> the second, in which the addressee thought one of two terms validated a given predication and the restriction must invert this opinion;
> the third, in which the addressee hesitated between which of two terms validated a predication and the restriction gives him or her an answer. Of course there is a preferred form for expressing restriction according to which of these situations corresponds to the addressee's state of mind.

INTER-UTTERANCE RELATIONSHIPS

Although rhetoricians devoted much of their efforts to the study of utterances, they never forgot that the isolated utterance is but an artifact, and that the reality which they had to account for was utterances linked together to make up texts. They consequently concentrated on inter-utterance relationships and they studied with particular care when, in an Arabic text, two utterances follow each other without coordination and when coordination is felt to be necessary. As a result the part of the treatises on rhetoric devoted to these questions is called 'the chapter of conjunction and disjunction'.

Disjunction between successive sentences in a text is not, in Arabic prose, such a simple matter as it may seem. There is, of course, the trivial case when there is disjunction simply because there is no relationship at all between the two successive sentences: this case is what Arab rhetoricians call 'complete separation' (*tamām al-inqiṭāʿ*). But there are many cases when disjunction is to be found between sentences presenting much in common. The most extreme case, called 'complete connectedness' (*tamām al-ittiṣāl*), is when the two sentences completely agree in formal structure and semantic content, the second one being almost a continuation of the first. It is, for example, the case between the two hemistichs of this verse of al-Mutanabbī:

wa-mā d-dahru 'illā min ruwāti qaṣā'idī
'iḏā qultu šiʿran 'aṣbaḥa d-dahru munšidā

Time is nothing but a reciter of my verses
when I say a poem time starts reciting

There is also an intermediate case when the two sentences are said to be in a relationship of 'near-complete connectedness' (*šibh tamām al-ittiṣāl*) because there exists a natural semantic relationship between them, as, for example, that obtaining between question and answer. An instance of this is to be found in the following verse:

qāla lī kayfa 'anta qultu ʿalīlū
sahrun dā'imun wa-ḥuznun ṭawīlū

He asked me 'how are you?' I said bad
endless insomnia and long sadness

As for conjunction, it has, in Arabic, three general markers: [wa], [fa], and [ṯumma]. The second always implies a meaning of succession (*tartīb*), temporal or logical, and the third adds to that same meaning that of mediateness (*tarāxī*). Consequently it is not very difficult to determine when the last two coordinative particles should be used. The matter is quite different with the first one because it has, in itself, only the pure and abstract meaning of 'associating' (*taŝrīk*). That is why the study of the conditions of conjunction is almost entirely centred on the analysis of the uses of [*wa*], which is, somehow, considered as the conjunctive particle *par excellence*.

Two major cases are analysed as requiring the use of the conjunctive particle. The first is when two successive sentences are meant to be two terms fulfilling the same functional role in a predicative relationship. Such is the case in the following verse (again by al-Mutanabbī), as the two connected sentences are both specifying elements of the predicand 'place' (*mawḍiʿun*).

wa-li-s-sirri minnī mawḍiʿun lā yanālu-hū
nadīmun wa-lā yufḍī 'ilayhi šarābū

There is in me a place for secret unattainable
by the drinking companion and inaccessible to wine

The second case is when there is between the two sentences a parallelism of structure and a semantic relationship. A good example of this may be found in this verse by Abū l-ʿAtāhiya:

qad yudriku r-rāqidu l-hādī bi-raqdati-hī
wa-qad yaxību 'axū r-rawḥāti wa-d-dulaǧī

He may succeed he who lies sleeping quietly
and he may fail he who is restlessly wandering

In this example, the two hemistichs correspond to two sentences having the same formal structure, belonging both to the type of informative predication, and manifestly expressing two aspects of the same idea, namely that quietness does not necessarily mean failure and that agitation does not always lead to success. It is natural, consequently, that these two sentences should be related by the conjunctive particle.

PROPER AND FIGURATIVE MEANING

The question of proper and figurative meaning has always fascinated thinkers in the Arabo-Islamic culture. This was not for purely theoretical reasons: what we have already said about the conceptions of al-Zamaxšarī, and more generally of Muʿtazilī thinkers, regarding the attributes of God suggests that this question was a highly strategic one in the fields of theology and politics. To this could be added the controversies opposing the *ǧabriyya*, who considered that action attributed to creatures directly resulted in reality from God's will, and the *qadariyya* (among whom were Muʿtazilīs), who considered that man was the only originator of his actions and so responsible for them.

The problems relating to the study of proper and figurative meaning in language have received a great deal of attention in Arabic rhetoric. Generally a basic distinction was established between the study of figurative meaning in isolated words, which was considered as an essentially 'linguistic metaphor' (*maǧāz luġawī*), and its study in predication, which was considered as a purely 'intellectual metaphor' (*maǧāz ʿaqlī*).

But this distinction is rather artificial, as clearly appears from the fact that the main results arrived at in both fields are essentially the same.

There are two basic ideas concerning the recognition and interpretation of metaphoric meaning. The first is that this meaning is not immediately understandable to the usual speaker of the language, and that it needs a contextual or situational hint manifesting that it is not the proper meaning, that which immediately pops up in the mind, which is intended. The second is that there must exist a relationship (*ʿalāqa*) between the proper meaning of a form used metaphorically, and the particular meaning intended. It is through the identification of that relationship that the addressee may understand the meaning aimed at by the speaker.

The number of possible relationships is rather limited. The major ones for nominals are:

the part/whole relationship, as in Qur'ān (4, 92) 'then freeing a believing neck', where the Arabic word for 'neck' is used to mean 'human being';
the cause/consequence relationship, as in Qur'ān (48, 10)

'God's hand is above their hands', where the Arabic for 'hand' stands for 'power', for the power is the cause of the hand's intervention;
the consequence/cause relationship, as in Qur'ān (4, 10) 'Indeed those who unjustly eat the wealth of orphans are only eating in their stomachs fire', where 'fire' is the ultimate consequence of the condemned action;
the location relationship, as in Qur'ān (96, 17) 'let him call his circle', meaning those who assemble in it.

For predicative structures the scope is somewhat wider, as it includes all the possible concepts organized around the predicate. One may find, for example, constructions as 'a sleepless night' (*layla sāhira*) meaning 'a night where no sleeping took place', or expressions like 'a satisfied life' (*ʿīša rāḍiya*) meaning 'a satisfying life'. What makes it possible to present the night as sleepless or the life as satisfied is that the predicates involved potentially entail the presence of these notions.

7

METRICS

PRELIMINARIES

To understand the theory of Arab metrics worked out by al-Xalīl, it is necessary to have some general notions about Arab poetry and metrics. The classical verse (*bayt*) is composed of two hemistichs (*miṣraʿ* or *šaṭr*). The hemistich is composed of two to four feet (*tafʿīl* or *juzʾ*). The foot is composed of syllables which are either short (u), or long (–). The last syllable of the hemistich is always long. A short syllable is composed of a consonant and a short vowel. All other syllables are long. What is known as a superheavy (CVVC or CVGC), which appears in words such as *qārratun*, is not authorized in poetry, except in certain rhymes.

The foot is not a non-structured sequence of syllables; on the contrary, it is composed of a stable disyllabic nucleus that the Arab metricians called *watid*, and of one or two syllables. This disyllabic nucleus can comprise either a short and a long syllable: u– (*watid mağmūʿ*), the iambus of classical metrics, or a long and a short syllable: –u (*watid mafrūq*), the trochee. Within a foot, the nucleus can be at the beginning, middle or end. We can summarize these data in the diagram on p. 138.

Classical verses are derived from sixteen metres. Table 7.1 gives, at a rather abstract level of representation, the list of these sixteen models of verse. The elements in square brackets are the stable ones, iambuses ([u–]) and trochees ([–u]), which the Arab metricians called *watid mağmūʿ* and *mafrūq*. The dot indicates a syllabic position which occurs in the verse as a short (u) or a long (–) syllable. The parentheses indicate that the foot which is included does not necessarily form part of the verse. The obliques mean that the corresponding foot may not be instantiated. As in

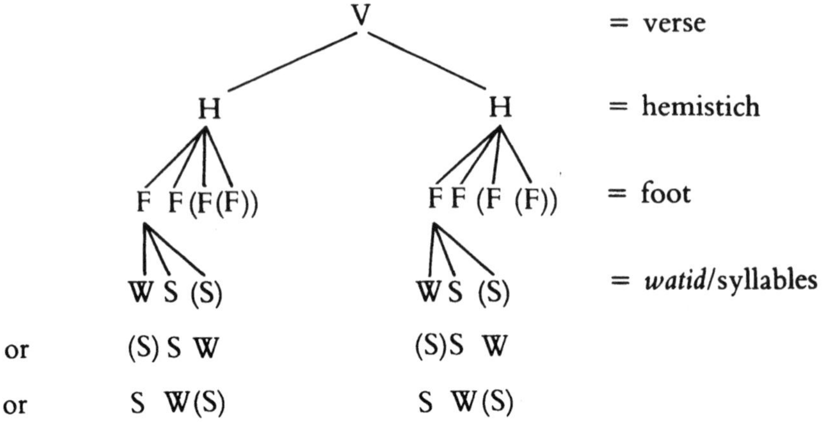

Table 7.1 The metres of Classical Arabic poetry

F1	*F2*	*F3*	*F4*		
I *Watid* in the beginning of the foot					
[u–]. .	[u–]. .	////	////	*hazaǧ*	1
[u–]{uu / –}–	[u–]{uu / –}–	([u–]–)	////	*wāfir*	2
[u–]. .	[–u]. .	////	////	*muḍāriʿ*	3
[u–].	[u–]. .	[u–].	[u–]. .	*ṭawīl*	4
[u–].	[u–].	[u–].	([u–].)	*mutaqārib*	5
II *Watid* in the end of the foot					
. .[u–]	. .[u–]	(. .[u–])	////	*raǧaz*	6
. .[u–]	. .[u–]	{uu– / –u– / ––}	////	*sarīʿ*	7
{uu / –} – [u–]	{uu / –} –[u–]	({uu / –}–[u–])	////	*kāmil*	8
. .[u–]	. .[–u]	. .[u–]	////	*munsariḥ*	9
. .[–u]	. .[u–]	////	////	*muqtaḍab*	10
. .[u–]	.[u–]	. .[u–]	(.[u–])	*basīṭ*	11
.[u–]	.[u–]	.[u–]	(.[u–])	*mutadārak*	12
III *Watid* in the middle of the foot					
.[u–].	.[u–].	(.[u–].)	////	*ramal*	13
.[u–].	.[–u].	(.[u–].)	////	*xafīf*	14
.[–u].	.[u–].	/////	////	*muǧtaṯṯ*	15
.[u–].	.[u–]	.[u–].	////	*madīd*	16

Bohas (1974) the metres are divided into three classes, according to whether the stable element is at the beginning, the middle, or the end of the foot. In lines 2 and 8 of Table 7.1, we mean by $\left\{\begin{matrix}uu\\-\end{matrix}\right\}-$ that one can find in this place in the verse either uu– or —. The difference between line 6 and 7 lies in the composition of the last foot: if F3 reproduces one of the sequences which occur in 7, then the verse should be attached to the *sarīʿ*, or else to the *raǧaz*. This table contains all the models of classical verse and each classical verse is the realization of one of these models. In other words, by starting from any line of the table and taking into account the convention concerning the realization of the dots, a classical verse is arrived at. Let us take, for example, line 14, and develop it:

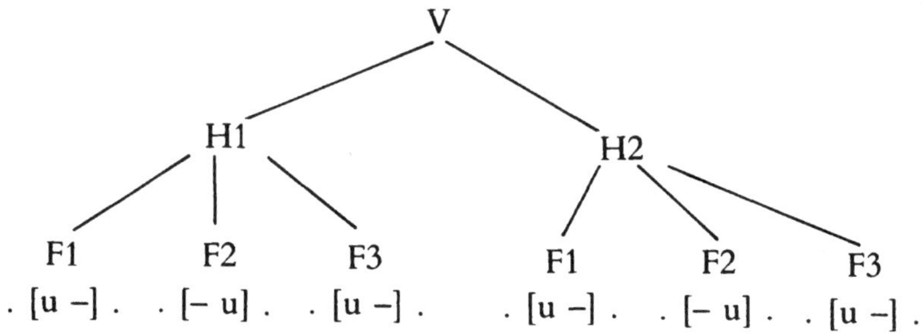

Let us suppose that all the dots are realized as:

– [u –] – – [– u] – – [u] – – [u –]– – [– u]– –[u –] –

we obtain the following verse:

H1 – [u –] – – [– u] – – [u –] –
lay/ta/ḥad̲/d̲ī/min/hū/wa/min/mit̲/li/hī/ʼan

H2 – [u –] – – [– u] – – [u –] –
lā/ta/rā/hū/ʿay/ nī/wa/ʼan/lā/ya/ rā/nī

One can of course carry out the operation in reverse: start from a verse and identify the metre, following the procedure proposed by Bohas (1974).

Finally, all the lines of a poem are based on the same metre, which means that at an abstract level they all have the same structure.

These preliminary notions will enable us to make a certain number of observations, observations which should be explained by all grammars of Arab metrics. Subsequently we shall be able to see how Arab metricians explained these realizations and to attempt a description of their system.

OBSERVATIONS

Referring again to Table 7.1 and paying particular attention to group II, one cannot fail to notice that all the metres in this group have common characteristics. That is immediately obvious for the *rağaz* and the *sarīʿ*, which only differ in respect of the last foot. Let us compare the *rağaz* and the *munsariḥ*: in these two metres the structure of the feet is identical, it is composed of two dots and one *watid*: . .W. The only difference between the two is that the *munsariḥ* includes a *watid mafrūq* in the second foot. Let us now compare the first two feet of the *rağaz* and of the *muqtaḍab*: the difference between the two sequences is once again due to the presence of a *watid mafrūq*, this time in the first foot. There is, therefore, an obvious relationship between the three metres and what naturally comes to mind is that the *munsariḥ* and the *muqtaḍab* can be derived from the *rağaz*, provided that one formulates the relationship ([u–] → [–u]) that has been noted.

Let us go on now to the *rağaz* and the *basīṭ*: the odd-numbered feet of the second are strictly identical to those of the former, since they are all composed of . .[u–]. As for the even-numbered, they are distinguished from the others by the lack of a dot. Here again, what becomes apparent is that the *basīṭ* can be derived from the *rağaz* by erasure of a dot, one foot out of every two. Furthermore, if this erasure occurs in all the feet, one obtains the *mutadārak*; but then we are obliged to note that there is a relationship between the erasure of a dot and the number of feet per hemistich: in all the tetrapods, there has been erasure in at least one foot out of two. Finally, the *kāmil* can be made up of feet which are strictly identical to those of the *rağaz*: ––u–, since, for the latter, the two dots may be realized in –. The relationship between the two metres can thus be characterized in the following manner: if all the dots are realized as – and subsequently one applies a diaeresis relationship (– → uu) which makes –– and uu– equivalent, then it is possible to derive the *kāmil* from the *rağaz*.

These three relationships, trochaization, erasure, and diaeresis, which we have just noted in group II, are found again in the other two groups. In group I, we can observe that the *wāfir* is to the *hazağ* what the *kāmil* is to the *rağaz*; that the *muḍāri'* is to the *hazağ* what the *munsariḥ* is to the *rağaz*; that the *ṭawīl* is to the *hazağ* what the *basīṭ* is to the *rağaz*; and that the *mutaqārib* is to the *hazağ* what the *mutadārak* is to the *rağaz*.

The same can be said of the third group by comparing the pairs:

> *ramal/xafīf* and *rağaz/munsariḥ*: presence of [–u] in the second foot;
> *ramal/muğtaṯṯ* and *rağaz/muqtaḍab*: presence of [–u] in the first foot;
> *ramal/madīd* and *rağaz/basīṭ*: erasure of dot one foot out of two.

In the three groups there are, therefore, relationships of the same type, which can be reduced to:

> trochaization: [u–] → [–u];
> erasure/tetrapody: . → ∅;
> diaeresis: – – → uu– (for the latter, the contiguity of the two – elements is necessary, which excludes its being carried out in group III.

Let us come now to the three metres: *rağaz*, *hazağ*, and *ramal*. They have two dots and a [u–] in their feet; only the position of the *watid* is different, and they can therefore be derived one from the other. This derivation can, for example, be carried out by cyclic permutation: if we start from a . .[u–] structure and if the *watid* is placed in the middle of the . . , one obtains the *ramal* (. [u–] .); if it is placed beyond the two dots, one obtains the *hazağ* ([u–]. .), which can be shown in the schema in Figure 7.1, taken from Bohas (1974).

We can therefore expect any grammar of Arabic metrics to explain these relationships in an explicit fashion, in other words, to describe the system. Furthermore, it must generate all the grammatical verses: in other words, link the system to the reality which is constituted by the corpus of Classical Arabic poetry. We are now going to see how the Arabic metric tradition answers these questions.

THE XALĪLIAN CIRCLES

For the tradition of the Arab metricians, which is based on the work by al-Xalīl, the metres are grouped in five circles. All the

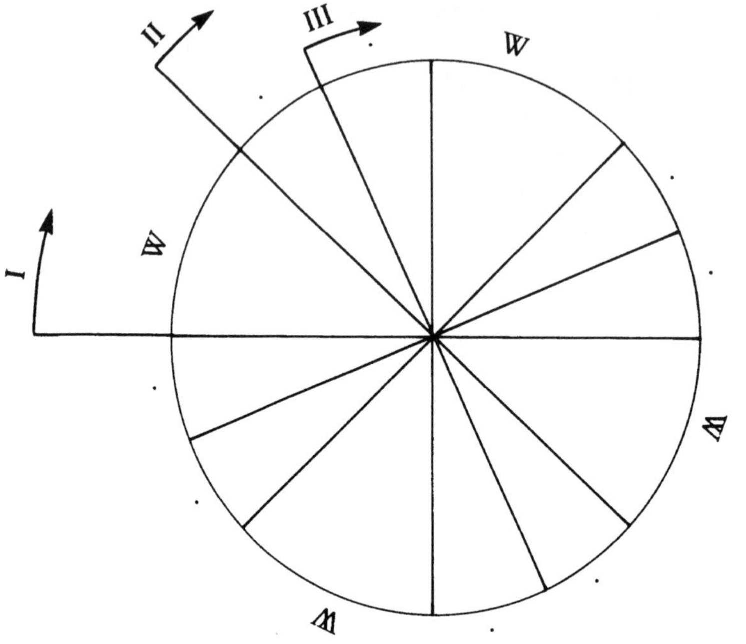

Figure 7.1 Cyclical permutation of metrical units

metres in the same circle share a common property:

1 *ṭawīl, madīd, basīṭ*: four feet and, alternatively, 2 dots/1 dot;
2 *wāfir, kāmil*: possibility of uu instead of one –;
3 *hazağ, rağaz, ramal*: all the feet have 2 dots and all the stable elements are [u–];
4 *sarīʿ, munsariḥ, xafīf, muḍāriʿ, muqtaḍab, muğtaṯṯ*: one of the stable elements is [–u];
5 *mutaqārib, mutadārak*: in all the feet there is only one dot.

Once again we find all the relationships observed above:

circle 1: erasure of one foot out of two;
circle 2: diaeresis;
circle 3: neither erasure, nor diaeresis, nor trochaization;
circle 4: trochaization;
circle 5: erasure in all feet.

Why were these groups called circles? Because all the members of a single group can be derived one from another by cyclic permutation, as can be seen in Figure 7.1, above; it remains to be seen how this permutation is effected technically in the Xalīlian system.

The level of representation of the metre noted by al-Xalīl is only made up of *watid* and long syllables (except as regards circle 2), but these elements are not noted in terms of long or short syllables, but in terms of segments, followed by vowels (i.e. CV), symbolized by 'o', and not followed by vowels (i.e. C), symbolized by '/'. It is possible that the o is the stylized form of the 'm' of *mutaḥarrik*, and the / the stylized form of the 's' of *sākin*. In order to avoid all confusion, we should point out that in certain modern treatises, the same symbolism is used with exactly opposite values: / for *mutaḥarrik* and o for *sākin*. These minimal units are grouped in:

sabab xafīf = o + / e.g. *mus*, i.e. –
sabab t̲aqīl = o + o e.g. *lima*, i.e. u u
watid mağmū' = o + o + / e.g. *'ağal*, i.e. u –
watid mafrūq = o + / + o e.g. *kayfa*, i.e. – u

It can be seen that in this inventory nothing corresponds to the short syllable (u) of Greek and Latin metrics. Hence, the *rağaz* will have the representation:

o/o/oo/ o/o/oo/ o/o/oo/ o/o/oo/ o/o/oo/ o/o/oo/

To make memorization of this sequence possible, and to give the division into feet immediately, use has been made of the root F'L and its derivates, as in morphology and phonology, which gives:

mustaf'ilun mustaf'ilun mustaf'ilun
o /o/ o o/ o /o /o o/ o/ o/ o o/

twice and notes, in terms of short/long syllables, a representation:

– – u – – – u – – – u –

The inventory of the feet in terms of F'L is the following (with the corresponding analysis in minimal units):

fa'uwlun	= [u–]–
fa''ilun	= –[u–]
mafa''iylun	= [u–]––
mustaf'ilun	= ––[u–]
fa''ila''tun	= –[u–]–
mufa''alatun	= [u–]uu–

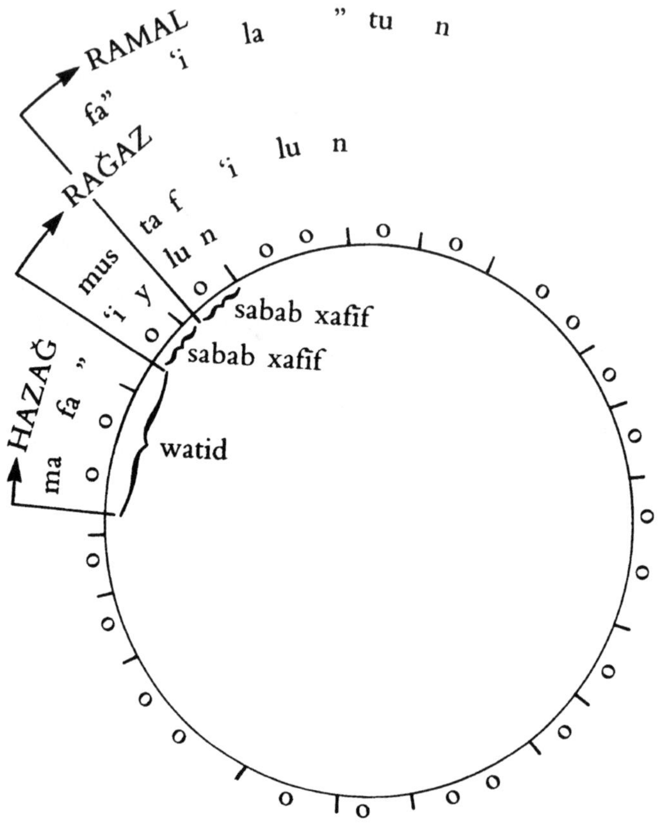

Figure 7.2 Al-Xalīl's third circle

mutafa''ʿilun = uu–[u–]
fa''ʿi la''tun = [–u]––
mafʿuwla''tu = ––[–u]
mustafʿi lun = –[–u]–

In the Xalīlian notation, circle 3 in Figure 7.1 is written as in Figure 7.2.

In this sequence, which is composed overwhelmingly of long syllables, the short syllable (the *watid* one), that is in the Xalīlian alphabet the sequence oo, constitutes the prominent element, and it is doubtless for this reason that, in the circles, one starts from the *watid* which constitutes the stable element of the foot, and subsequently rotates, as is shown in Figure 7.2. This makes it possible to ģenerate:

mafa"ʿiylun six times = *hazağ*
mustafʿilun six times = *rağaz*
fa"ʿila"tun six times = *ramal*

THE ZIḤĀFĀT

But we know, in fact, that lines of poetry can have short or long syllables instead of these long syllables (i.e. in the places noted as dots in Table 7.1). Thus the first foot of a *rağaz* verse has four possibilities: u– u– , uuu–, –uu–, and ––u–. Seeing that the level of the metre only includes long syllables (––u–), in a notation which is limited to segmental units (o/o/oo/), all the sequences where short syllables appear are derived by elision rules called *ziḥāfāt*, which essentially erase an element in a certain context; thus, from o/o/oo/ = – – u– , one obtains:

Ø = u – u–
  Ø = – u u–
Ø Ø = u u u–

that is, by using the notation FʿL:

mustafʿilun	A	B
Ø	= *mutafʿilun*	= *mafa"ʿilun*
Ø	= *mustaʿilun*	= *muftaʿilun*
Ø Ø	= *mutaʿilun*	= *faʿalatun*

In column A the result of the rule of erasure is given, but as this result, for example *mutafʿilun*, is close to the configuration of the basic foot *mafa"ʿiylun*, it is named *mafa"ʿilun*, and so on for column B. Each of these erasure rules has a name, in accordance with the place to which they apply in the foot:

xabn: erasure of the second consonant not followed by a vowel,

e.g.: *fa"ʿilun* → *faʿilun*
1 23 4 5

i.e.: –[u–] → u[u–]

waqṣ: erasure of the second consonant followed by a vowel,

e.g.: *mutafa''ʿilun* → *mufa''ʿilun*. The consonant is erased with
1 2 3 4 567 its vowel.

i.e.: uu–[u–] → u–[u–]

'iḍmār: erasure of the vowel of the second consonant,

e.g.: *mutafa''ʿilun* → *mutfa''ʿilun* = *mustafʿilun*
1 234567

i.e.: uu–[u–] → ––[u–]

qabḍ: erasure of the fifth consonant not followed by a vowel,

e.g.: *mafa''ʿiylun* → *mafa''ʿilun*
1 2345 67

i.e.: [u–]–– → [u–]u–

ʿaql: erasure of the fifth consonant with the vowel which follows it,

e.g.: *mufa''ʿalatun* → *mufa''ʿatun* = *mafa''ʿilun*
1 2 3456 7

i.e.: [u–]uu– → [u–]u–

ʿaṣb: erasure of the vowel of the fifth consonant,

e.g.: *mufa''ʿalatun* → *mufa''ʿaltun* = *mafa''ʿiylun*
1 23456 7

i.e.: [u–]uu– → [u–]––

ṭayy: erasure of the fourth consonant not followed by a vowel,

e.g.: *mustafʿilun* → *mustaʿilun* = *muftaʿilun*
1 234567

i.e.: ––[u–] → –u[u–]

kaff: erasure of the seventh consonant not followed by a vowel,

e.g.: *mafa"ʿiylun* → *mafa"ʿiylu*
1 2 3456 7

i.e.: [u–]–– → [u–]–u

Two *ziḥāfāt* can affect a foot simultaneously, thus:

xabl = *xabn* + *ṭayy*

e.g.: *mustafʿilun* → *mutaʿilun* = *faʿalatun*
1 23456 7

i.e.: ––[u–] → uu[u–]

xazl = *'iḍmār* + *ṭayy*

e.g.: *mutafa"ʿilun* → *mutfaʿilun* = *muftaʿilun*
1 2 34567

i.e.: uu–[u–] → –u[u–]

šakl = *xabn* + *kaff*

e.g.: *fa"ʿila"tun* → *faʿila"tu*
1 23456 7

i.e.: –[u–]– → u[u–]u

naqṣ = *ʿaṣb* + *kaff*

e.g.: *mufa"ʿalatun* → *mufa"ʿaltu* = *mafa"ʿiylu*

i.e.: [u–]uu– → [u–]–u

Besides these transformations, which affect the internal feet of the verse (*ḥašw*), another set of rules affects the last foot of the hemistich (*ʿarūḍ*) and of the verse (*ḍarb*). These are the *ʿilal*, which must be applied in the same way to all lines of the poem.

The formulation of the *ʿilal* would not teach us anything further about the Xalīlian system, so we will, rather, devote the rest of this paragraph to the problem of the compatibility of the *ziḥāfāt*. Let us return to Table 7.1 and consider line 13:

F1	F2	F3	F4
.[u–].	.[u–].	(.[u–].)	////

We have seen that each dot can be rewritten as – or u, but certain sequences of u are illicit. Let us systematically develop F1 and F2:

	F1	F2
	.[u–].	.[u–].
OK	.[u–]u	– [u–].
OK	.[u–]–	– [u–].
OK	.[u–]–	u [u–]
★	.[u–]u	u [u–].

In order to exclude this sequence and others comparable to it, the Arab metricians (who, let us remember, start off with abstract representations comprising long syllables, noted in segmental units, that is:

F1	F2		F1 F2
– [u–] –	– [u–]–	=	o / o o/ o / o / o o/ o/
		=	fa" ʿila' *tun fa* " ʿila"tun

prohibit the simultaneous application of the *ziḥāfāt* (*muʿāqaba*) in the two underlined *sabab*, thus, *tun fa* (= –u) and *tu fa"* (= u–) will be allowed, but not *tu fa*, i.e. u u. This fact is justified by a prohibition which reminds us somewhat of the prohibition of the four CV in phonology which prevents the occurrence of a sequence of four CV distributed over two feet. One can go through the entire classical poetical production and verify an empirical generalization: the sequences of four CV distributed over two feet are banned, whereas they are allowed within a single foot. We can find in the metricians' writings what had already been noted about the grammarians: the precision and wealth of technical terminology, which makes it possible to describe precisely the least empirical detail, is connected with the concern about justifying the application or non-application of the rules by having recourse to general observations.

OVERGENERATION IN THE XALĪLIAN SYSTEM

This system makes it possible to generate all existing verses, but it also generates a certain number of others, and that mainly for two reasons. First, the metres are grouped in circles, according to the common property which they share; that leads, for example, to the inclusion of the *muǧtaṯṯ* and the *xafīf* in the same circle, whereas the former never has more than two feet per hemistich and the other can have three. The solution adopted by the Arab metricians to overcome this difficulty is to say that the *muǧtaṯṯ* in the system (*fī l-aṣl*) comprises three feet, but that the third foot is always erased (*maǧzū' dā'iman*).

The second reason for the overgeneration of the system lies in the very way the circles function. Let us consider the first one, called *al-muxtalif*, which includes the *ṭawīl*, the *basīṭ*, and the *madīd* (it may be mentioned in passing that the latter constitutes an example of the first case of overgeneration: it is generated by the system with four feet, but, in fact, it never has more than three). Figure 7.3 makes it possible to show that the circle generates five

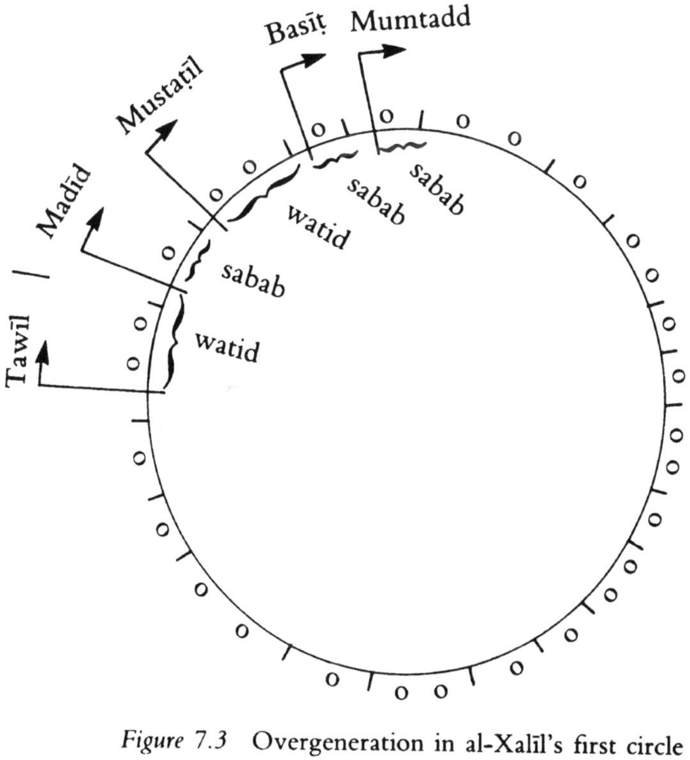

Figure 7.3 Overgeneration in al-Xalīl's first circle

metres, the *mumtadd* and the *mustaṭīl* being added to the three we have mentioned. But for the Arab grammarians, overgeneration was never considered, in metrics or in morphology, to be a fault, the non-attested forms (*muhmal*) being quite as consistent with the laws of the system as those which have actually been realized.

THE ORIENTALISTS AND THE XALĪLIAN SYSTEM

The Xalīlian metrics, of which we have just attempted to give a rapid description, has been the subject of various commentaries by orientalists. It is of course not possible to summarize here all the opinions of the latter. A summary can be found in Weil (1960). Certain points can none the less be mentioned. What seems to have embarrassed these scholars most are the following facts.

1 Arabic metrics do not entail the concept of the syllable. It is clear that the grammarians managed very well without it in morphology and phonology, and that did not prevent them from giving us penetrating analyses of their language. But some have wondered whether it could not be said that the grammarians and metricians had somewhere deep down the notion of the syllable.

A humorous answer might be: one may very well suppose that Chomsky and Halle had somewhere deep down the notion of the syllable, but this does not make the syllable part of the formalism of the standard theory. Another way of looking at the problem consists in going beyond the gap in the terminology to state that the necessity of metrical analysis led the Arab grammarians to postulate suprasegmental structures, whether they correspond with the western conception of the syllable or not: an outline of this approach can be found in Kouloughli (1986) and above, p. 95.

2 Arabic metrics did not entail the notion of metrical stress (*ictus*). That has distressed a lot of people. Some have concluded, prematurely, that stress played no part in Arabic metrics; others have attempted to find the notion of *ictus* somewhere in the circles and, Heaven knows, at least if we have understood anything, it does not appear there! If the grammarians did not speak about stress, and the metricians did not speak about *ictus*, that need not distress us: these suprasegmental phenomena have been trans-

mitted by oral tradition and it is by referring to it that we can speak about them. Let us compare metrics with a field in which the oral tradition plays a big part: what would we know of the *tartīl* of the Qur'ān if we had only the reading marks of the Qur'ānic text at our disposal? Or what would we know of the *tajwīd* if we only had specialized treatises? Similarly, there is a tradition of declaiming poetry, and it is by analysing the suprasegmental phenomena within that framework that we can hope to progress, while, of course, correlating our analysis with the collection of facts which we know, but without asking the Arab grammarians and metricians to treat points which did not fall within their province; that would be as absurd as to reproach specialists of the *naḥw* for not treating figures of speech, when this field belonged to the rhetoricians.

BIBLIOGRAPHY

Two general bibliographies may be consulted:

DIEM, W. (1981) 'Bibliography, Sekundärliteratur zur einhimischen arabischen Grammatik Schreibung', *Historiographia Linguistica*, 8.

VERSTEEGH, C.H.M. (1983) 'Current bibliography on the history of Arabic grammar', *Journal of Arabic Linguistics*, 10.

A SELECTION

We will first cite twelve works with brief comments. Each of these titles represents a certain approach to the AGs' texts.

ARNALDEZ, R.(1956) *Grammaire et théologie chez Ibn Hazm de Cordoue. Essai sur la structure et les conditions de la pensée musulmane*, Paris: Vrin. The study of grammarians' texts by a philosopher, in particular the works of the Ẓāhirites in Spain. Grammar and logic.

BOHAS, G. and GUILLAUME, J.-P. (1984) *Etude des théories des grammairiens arabes*, I: *Morphologie et phonologie*, Damas: Institut français.
An attempt at an explanation of the methods of the Arab grammarians in the field of *taṣrīf*. First lengthy work written from the point of view adopted in the present book.

CARTER, M.G. (1972) Les Origines de la grammaire arabe. *Revue des Etudes Islamiques*, 49.
A brilliant refutation of the theses about the Greek origin of Arabic grammar. The radical originality of the *Kitāb* of Sībawayhi, the first great work about Arabic grammar. The role of juridical reasoning in grammatical argumentation.

CARTER, M.G.(1981) *Arab Linguistics, an introductory classical text with translation and notes*, Amsterdam: Benjamins.
A translated and annotated edition of the *Ājurrūmiyya*, one of the most famous pedagogical texts about grammar of the late period: a monument.

DE SACY, S.(1829) *Anthologie grammaticale arabe*, Paris: Imprimerie Royale.
The first large-scale work putting at the disposal of the non-Arabist public texts from the Arabic grammatical tradition.
DE SACY, S.(1831) *Grammaire arabe*, Paris: Imprimerie Royale.
This grammar is also an interpretation of the AGs' texts within the framework of the *Grammaire Générale*.
FLEISCH, H.(1961) *Traité de philologie arabe*, vol. 1: *Préliminaires, phonétique, morphologie*, Beirut: Imprimerie Catholique.
The first chapter is devoted to the method of the Arab grammarians and gives a good summary of the accepted opinions in this field. Throughout this book, as in Volume II, on every question the Arab grammarians' texts are explained and discussed, and it is possible to have a very precise idea about the evaluations of the orientalist linguists of this generation concerning the methods of the Arab grammarians.
GOGUYER, A.(1888) *La 'Alfiyyah d'Ibnu Mâlik, suivie de la Lâmiyya du même auteur*, Beirut: Imprimerie des Belles Lettres.
Translation of the famous grammatical poem with a technical lexicon. A reaction against the interpretation of De Sacy: 'By trying to compare this study to that of European syntax, especially at such a time when general syntax, still in its infancy today, was an unknown science, he only succeeded in spreading confusion in a system which was imperfect but at any rate very convenient and sanctioned by centuries of usage. The Arabs had a methodical syntax and a classification of the rules of government long before we did; we may do better than them, even in their own language, but first of all we must find out exactly what they did' (Introduction).
MEHIRI, A. (1973) *Les Théories grammaticales d'Ibn Ǧinni*, Université de Tunis.
An example of a standard 'Doctorat d'Etat' in the tradition of French Arabic scholars.
MERX, A.(1889) *Historia artis grammaticae apud Syros*, Leipzig.
Chapter IX constitutes the first basic work for the account of the hypothesis of the Greek origin of Arab grammar.
VERSTEEGH, C.H.M. (1977) *Greek Elements in Arabic Linguistic Thinking*, Leiden: Brill.
Re-examines the theses about Greek origin. More subtle and better informed than his predecessors. Contributes new elements concerning the possible influence of Stoic logic.
WEIL, G.(1913) *Abū l-Barakāt ibn al-Anbārī, Die Grammatischen Steitfragen der Basrer und Kufer*, Leiden: Brill.
Remained the definitive reference work on the question for half a century (see quotations from this and other works by this author in Fleisch, 1961).

REFERENCES

PRIMARY SOURCES

ABŪ L-TAYYIB, *Marātib* = ABŪ L-TAYYIB 'ABD AL-RAḤMĀN B. ALĪ AL-LUĠAWĪ, *Marātib al-naḥwiyyīn*, ed. Muḥammad Abū l-Faḍl Ibrāhīm, Cairo: Dār al-Nahḍa, 1954.

IBN ǦINNĪ, *Xaṣā'iṣ* = ABŪ L-FATḤ 'UṮMĀN IBN ǦINNĪ, *Al-Xaṣā'iṣ*, ed. Muḥammad Alī al-Naǧǧār, Cairo. 1952–6; repr. Beirut: Dār al-Hudā, n.d.

IBN ǦINNĪ, *Sirr* = ABŪ L-FATḤ 'UṮMĀN IBN ǦINNĪ, *Sirr ṣinā'at al-i'rāb*, ed. Muṣṭafā al-Saqqā', Ibrāhīm Muṣṭafā, Muḥammad al-Zafzāf and 'Abd Allāh Amīn, vol. 1, Cairo: Muṣṭafā al-Bābī al-Ḥalabī, 1954.

IBN ǦINNĪ, *Mulūkī* = ABŪ L-FATḤ 'UṮMĀN IBN ǦINNĪ, *Taṣrīf al-mulūkī*, in Ibn Ya'īš, *Šarḥ al-Mulūkī* = MUWAFFAQ AL-DIN ABU L-BARĀ' YA'ĪŠ IBN YA'ĪŠ: *Šarḥ al-Mulūkī fī l-taṣrīf*, ed. Faxr al-Dīn Qabāwa, Aleppo: al-Maktaba al-'Arabiyya, 1973.

IBN ǦINNĪ, *Munṣif* = ABŪ L-FATḤ 'UṮMĀN IBN ǦINNĪ, *Al-Munṣif*, ed. Ibrāhīm Muṣṭafā and 'Abdallah Amīn, Cairo: Muṣṭafā al-Bābī al-Ḥalabī, 1952–60.

IBN AL-SARRĀǦ, *Uṣūl* = ABŪ BAKR MUḤAMMAD B. AL-SARĪ IBN AL-SARRĀǦ, *Kitāb al-uṣūl fī l-naḥw*, ed. 'Abd al-Ḥusayn al-Fatlī, vol. 1, al-Naǧaf, 1973; vol. 2 Baghdad, 1973; repr. Beirut: Mu'assasat al-Risāla, 1985.

IBN SĪNĀ, *Asbāb* = ABŪ 'ALĪ AL-ḤUSAYN IBN SĪNĀ, *Asbāb ḥudūṯ al-ḥurūf*, Cairo: al-Maktaba al-Salafiyya, 1353 h.

IBN 'UṢFŪR, *Al-Mumti'* = ABŪ L-'ABBĀS 'ALI B. MU'MIN IBN 'UṢFŪR AL-IŠBĪLĪ, *Al-Mumti' fī t-taṣrīf*, ed. Faxr al-Dīn Qabāwa, Aleppo: al-Maktaba al-'Arabiyya, 1970.

IBN 'AQĪL, *Šarḥ* = BAHĀ' AL-DĪN 'ABDALLĀH IBN 'AQĪL, *Šarḥ al-Alfiyya*, ed. Muḥammad Muḥyī l-Dīn 'Abd al-Ḥamīd, 14th edn, Cairo: al-Maktaba al-Tiǧāriyya al-Kubrā, 1964.

IBN QUTAYBA, *Ši'r wa-l-šu'arā'* = ABU MUHAMMAD 'ABDALLAH B. MUSLIM IBN QUTAYBA AL-DĪNAWARĪ, *Kitāb al-ši'r wa-l-šu'arā'(al-muqaddima)*, ed. Aḥmad Muḥammad Šākir, Cairo: Dār al-Ma'ārif, 1966, 1967.

IBN QUTAYBA, *Adab al-kātib* = ABŪ MUHAMMAD 'ABDALLĀH B. MUSLIM IBN QUTAYBA AL-DĪNAWARĪ, *Kitāb adab al-kātib*, ed. Max Grünert. Leiden: Brill, 1900; repr. Beirut: Dār Ṣādir, 1967.

IBN MADĀ', *Radd* = ABŪ L-'ABBĀS AHMAD IBN MADĀ' AL-QURṬUBĪ, *Kitāb al-radd 'alā l-nuḥāt*, ed. Šawqi Ḍayf, Cairo: Dār al-Fikr al-'Arabī, 1947; repr. Cairo: Dār al-Ma'ārif 1982.

IBN AL-MU'TAZZ, *Badī'* = 'ABDALLĀH IBN AL-MU'TAZZ, *Kitāb al-badī'*, ed. Ignatius Kratchkovsky, London: Luzac, 1935; repr. Baghdad: Maktabat al-Muṯannā, 1967.

IBN MĀLIK, *Alfiyya* = ĞAMĀL AL-DĪN ABŪ 'ABDALLĀH MUḤAMMAD IBN MĀLIK, *Al-Alfiyya*, ed. Antonin Goguyer *La 'Alfiyyah d'Ibnu Mâlik, suivie de la Lâmiyya du même auteur*, Beirut: Imprimerie des Belles Lettres, 1888.

IBN HIŠĀM, *Awḍaḥ al-masālik* = ĞAMĀL AL-DĪN ABŪ MUḤAMMAD 'ABDALLĀH B. YŪSUF IBN HIŠĀM, *Awḍaḥ al-masālik ilā Alfiyyat Ibn Mālik*, ed. Muḥammad Muḥyī l-Dīn 'Abd al-Ḥamīd, Cairo: Matba'at al-Sa'āda, 1967.

IBN HIŠĀM, *Muġnī l-labīb* = ĞAMĀL AL-DĪN ABŪ MUḤAMMAD 'ABDALLĀH B. YŪSUF IBN HIŠĀM, *Muġnī l-labīb 'an kutub al-a'ārīb*, ed. Māzin al-Mubārak and Muḥammad 'Alī Ḥamd Allāh, Beirut: Dār al-Fikr, 1972.

IBN HIŠĀM, *Qaṭr al-nadā* = ĞAMĀL AL-DĪN ABŪ MUḤAMMAD 'ABDALLĀH B. YŪSUF IBN HIŠĀM, *Šarḥ Qaṭr al-nadā*, ed. Muḥammad Muḥyī l-Dīn 'Abd al-Ḥamīd, Cairo: Maktabat al-Sa'āda, 1963.

IBN HIŠĀM, *Šaḏarāt al-ḏahab* = ĞAMĀL AL-DĪN ABŪ MUḤAMMAD 'ABDALLĀH B. YŪSUF IBN HIŠĀM, *Šarḥ Šaḏarāt al-ḏahab*, ed. Muḥammad Muḥyī l-Dīn 'Abd al-Ḥamīd, Cairo, 1945.

IBN WAHB, *Al-Burhān* = ABŪ L-HUSAYN ISḤĀQ B. IBRĀHĪM B. SULAYMĀN B. WAHB, *Al-Burhān fī wuğūh al-bayān*, ed. Aḥmad Maṭlūb and Xadīğā al-Ḥadīṯī, Baghdad, 1967.

IBN YA'ĪŠ, *Šarḥ al-Mulūkī* = MUWAFFAQ AL-DĪN ABŪ L-BARĀ' YA'ĪŠ IBN YA'ĪŠ, *Šarḥ al-Mulūkī fī l-taṣrīf*, ed. Faxr al-Dīn Qabāwa, Aleppo: al-Maktaba al-'Arabiyya, 1973.

IBN YA'ĪŠ, *Šarḥ al-Mufaṣṣal* = MUWAFFAQ AL-DĪN ABŪ L-BARĀ' YA'ĪŠ IBN YA'ĪŠ, *Šarḥ al-Mufaṣṣal*, Cairo: al-Maktaba al-Munīriyya, 1928–31.

AL-ASTARĀBĀḎĪ, *Šāfiya* = RAḌĪ L-DĪN MUḤAMMAD B. AL-HASAN AL-ASTARĀBĀḎĪ, *Šarḥ Šāfiyat Ibn al-Ḥāğib*, ed. Muḥammad Nūr al-Ḥasan, Muḥammad al-Zafzāf and Muḥyī l-Dīn 'Abd al-Ḥamīd, Cairo: al-Maktaba al-Tijāriyya al-Kubrā, 1939; repr. Beirut: Dār al-Kutub al-'Ilmiyya, 1975.

AL-ASTARĀBĀḎĪ, *Kāfiya* = RAḌĪ L-DĪN MUḤAMMAD B. AL-HASAN AL-ASTARĀBĀḎĪ, *Šarḥ al-Kāfiya fī l-naḥw*. Beirut: Dār al-Kutub al-'Ilmiyya, 1969.

AL-AŠMŪNĪ, *Šarḥ* = ABŪ L-ḤASAN NŪR AL-DĪN 'ALĪ B. MUḤAMMAD AL-AŠMŪNĪ, *Šarḥ al-Alfiyya*, in *Ḥāšiyat al Ṣabbān*. Cairo, n.d.

AL-AṢMA'Ī, *Fuḥūlat* = 'ABD AL-MALIK B. QURAYB B. 'ABD

AL-MALIK AL-AṢMAʿĪ, *Kitāb fuḥūlat al-šuʿarā'*, ed. Ch. C. Torrey, Beirut: Dār al-Kitāb al-Ǧadīd, 1971.

AL-ANBĀRĪ, *Inṣāf* = ABŪ L-BARAKĀT ʿABD AL-RAḤMĀN B. MUḤAMMAD AL-ANBĀRĪ, *Kitāb al-inṣāf fī masā'il al-xilāf bayna l-nahwiyyīn al-baṣriyyīn wa-l-kūfiyyīn*, ed. Gotthold Weil, Leiden: Brill, 1913.

AL-ANBĀRĪ, *Lumaʿ* = ABŪ L-BARAKĀT ʿABD AL-RAḤMĀN B. MUḤAMMAD AL-ANBĀRĪ, *al-Iġrāb fī ǧadal al-iʿrāb wa-Lumaʿ al-adilla fī uṣūl al- naḥw*, ed. Saʿīd al-Afġānī, Damascus: Dār al-Fikr, 1957; repr. Beirut, 1971.

AL-BĀQILLĀNĪ, *Iʿǧāz al-Qur'ān* = ABŪ BAKR MUḤAMMAD B. AL-TAYYIB AL-BĀQILLĀNĪ, *Iʿǧāz al-Qur'ān*, ed. Ahmad Ṣaqr, Cairo: Dār al-Maʿārif bi-Miṣr, 1954; repr. Cairo, 1971.

ṮAʿLAB, *Qawāʿid al-šiʿr* = ABŪ L-ʿABBĀS AḤMAD B. YAḤYĀ ṮAʿLAB, *Qawāʿid al-šiʿr*, ed. ʿAbd al-Tawwāb Ramaḍān, Cairo, 1966.

AL-ǦĀḤIẒ, *Bayān wa-l-tabyīn* = ABŪ ʿUṮMĀN B. BAHR B. MAḤBŪB AL-KINĀNĪ AL-ǦĀḤIẒ, *Kitāb al-bayān wa-l-tabyīn*, Beirut: Al-Šarika al-Lubnāniyya li-l-Kitāb, 1968.

AL-ǦURǦĀNĪ, *Dalā'il* = ABŪ BAKR ʿABD AL-QĀHIR B. ʿABD AL-RAḤMĀN AL-ǦURǦĀNĪ, *Dalā'il al-iʿǧāz fī ʿilm al-maʿānī*, ed. Muḥammad ʿAbduh, Maḥmūd al-Šanqīṭī, and Rašīd Riḍā, Cairo: Maktabat al-Qāhira, 1969; repr. Beirut: Dār al-Maʿārif, 1978.

AL-GUMAḤI, *Ṭabaqāt* = MUHAMMAD B. SALLĀM AL-ǦUMAḤĪ, *Ṭabaqāt fuḥūl al-šuʿarā'*, ed. J. Hell, Leiden: Brill, 1916.

ḤĀZIM AL-QARṬAǦANNĪ, *Minhāǧ al-bulaġa* = ABŪ L-ḤUSAYN ḤĀZIM AL-QARṬAǦANNĪ, *Minhāǧ al-bulaġa' wa-sirāǧ al-udabā'*, ed. Muḥammad al-Ḥabīb B. al-Xūǧa, Tunis: Dār al-Kutub al-Šarqiyya, 1966.

AL-XAṬṬĀBĪ, *Risāla fī iǧāz al-Qur'ān* = ABŪ SULAYMĀN ḤAMD B. MUḤAMMAD B. IBRĀHĪM AL-XAṬṬĀBĪ, 'Risāla fī bayān iʿǧāz al-Qur'ān', in *Ṯalāṯ rasā'il fī iǧāz al-Qur'ān*, ed. Muhammad Xalafallah and Muhammad Zaġlūl Salām, Cairo: Dār al-Maʿārif bi-Miṣr, 1956; repr. Cairo, 1968.

AL-XALĪL, *ʿAyn* = ABU ʿABD AL-RAḤMĀN AL-XALĪL B. AHMAD AL-FARĀHĪDĪ, *Kitāb al-ʿayn*, ed. Mahdī l-Maxzūmī and Ibrāhīm al-Sāmarrā'ī, Qom: Dār al-Hiǧra, 1405.

AL-RUMMĀNĪ, *Nukat* = ABŪ L-ḤASAN ʿALĪ B. ʿĪSĀ AL-RUMMĀNĪ, 'Al-Nukat fī iʿǧāz al-Qur'ān', in *Ṯalāṯ rasā'il fī iʿǧāz al-Qur'ān*, ed. Muhammad Xalafallah and Muhammad Zaġlūl Salām, Cairo: Dār al-Maʿārif bi-Miṣr, 1956; repr. Cairo, 1968.

AL-ZAǦǦĀǦĪ, *Īḍāḥ* = 'ABŪ L-QĀSIM AL-ZAǦǦĀǦĪ, *Kitāb al-īḍāḥ fī ʿilal al-nahw*, ed. Māzin al-Mubārak, Beirut: Dār al-Nafā'is, 1973.

AL-ZAMAXŠARĪ, *Asās al-balāġa* = ABŪ L-QĀSIM MAḤMŪD B. ʿUMAR AL-ZAMAXŠARĪ, *Asās al-balāġa*, Beirut: Dār Ṣādir, 1979.

AL-ZAMAXŠARĪ, *Kaššāf* = ABŪ L-QĀSIM MAḤMŪD B. ʿUMAR AL-ZAMAXŠARĪ, *Al-Kaššāf ʿan ḥaqā'iq ġawāmiḍ al-tanzīl wa-ʿuyūn al-aqāwīl fī wujūh al-ta'wīl*, Beirut: Dār al-Fikr, n.d.

SĪBAWAYHI, *Kitāb* = ABŪ BIŠR ʿAMR B. ʿUṮMĀN SĪBAWAYHI, *Al-Kitāb*, Cairo: Būlāq, 1898–1900.

AL-SAKKĀKĪ, *Miftāḥ al-'ulūm* = ABU YA'QŪB YŪSUF B. ABĪ BAKR MUḤAMMAD B. 'ALĪ AL-SAKKĀKĪ, *Kitāb miftāḥ al-'ulūm*, Cairo: al-Maṭba'a al-Adabiyya, 1317 A.H.

AL-SUYŪṬĪ, *Ham' al-hawāmi'* = ĞALĀL AL-DĪN ABŪ L-FAḌL 'ABD AL-RAḤMĀN AL-SUYŪṬĪ, *Ham' al-hawāmi' šarḥ Ğam' al-ğawāmi'*, Cairo: Dār al-Sa'āda, 1327 A.H.; repr. Beirut: Dār al-Ma'rifa, n.d.

AL-SUYŪṬĪ, *Iqtirāḥ'* = ĞALĀL AL-DĪN ABŪ L-FAḌL 'ABD AL-RAḤMĀN AL-SUYŪṬĪ, *Kitāb al-iqtirāḥ fī uṣūl al-naḥw*, ed. 'Aḥmad Muhammad Qāsim, Cairo: Maṭba'at al-Sa'āda, 1976.

AL-ŠĀFI'Ī, *Risāla* = MUḤAMMAD B. IDRĪS AL-ŠĀFI'Ī, *Al-Risāla fī 'ilm uṣūl al-fiqh*, ed. Aḥmad Muḥammad Šākir, no date or place specified.

'ABD AL-ĞABBĀR, *Muğnī* = ABŪ L-ḤASAN 'ABD AL-ĞABBĀR AL-ASADĀBĀDĪ, *Al-Muğnī fī abwāb al-tawḥīd wa-l-'adl*, vol. 16: *i'ğāz al-Qur'ān*, ed. Amīn al-Xūli, Cairo: Wizārat al-Ṯaqāfa, 1960.

AL-ĠAZĀLĪ, *Mustaṣfā* = ABŪ ḤĀMID B. MUḤAMMAD AL-ĠAZĀLĪ, *Al-Mustaṣfā fī 'ilm al-uṣūl*, Beirut: Dār al-Kutub al-'Ilmiyya, 1938.

AL-FARRĀ', *Ma'ānī l-Qur'ān* = ABŪ ZAKARIYYĀ YAHYĀ B. ZIYĀD, *Ma'ānī l-Qur'ān*, ed. 'Aḥmad Yūsuf Nağātī, Muḥammad 'Alī al-Nağğār and 'Abd al-Fattāḥ Ismā'īl Šalabī, Cairo, 1955–72; repr. Beirut: 'Ālam al-Kutub, 1980.

QUDĀMA B. ĞA'FAR, *Naqd al-ši'r* = ABŪ L-FARAĞ QUDĀMA B. ĞA'FAR, *Naqd al-ši'r*, ed. Kamāl Muṣṭafā, Baghdad: Maktabat al-Muṯannā, 1963.

AL-QAZWĪNĪ, *Talxīṣ* = ĞALĀL AL-DĪN MUHAMMAD B. 'ABD AL-RAḤMĀN AL-QAZWĪNĪ, *Al-Talxīṣ fī 'ulūm al-balāğa*, ed. 'Abd al-Raḥmān al-Barqūqī, Cairo: al-Maktaba al-Tijāriyya al-Kubrā, 1904; repr. Cairo, 1932.

AL-QAZWĪNĪ, *Īḍāḥ* = ĞALĀL AL-DĪN MUHAMMAD B. 'ABD AL-RAḤMĀN AL-QAZWĪNĪ, *Al-Īḍāḥ fī 'ulūm al-balāğa*, ed. 'Abd al-Mun'im al-Xafāğī, Cairo, 1949; repr. Beirut: Dār al-Kitāb al-Lubnānī, 1980.

AL-MUBARRAD, *Muqtaḍab* = ABŪ L-'ABBĀS MUḤAMMAD B. YAZĪD AL-MUBARRAD, *Kitāb al-muqtaḍab*, ed. Muḥammad 'Abd al-Xāliq 'Uḍayma, Cairo: Dār al-Taḥrīr, 1965–8.

SECONDARY SOURCES

AUROUX, S. (1986) 'Rapport d'habilitation', unpublished typescript, University of Paris-7.

BOHAS, G. (1974) 'La métrique arabe classique', *Linguistics*, 140.

BOHAS, G. and GUILLAUME, J.-P. (1984) *Etude des théories des grammairiens arabes*, vol. 1. *Morphologie et phonologie*, Damas: Institut français.

CARTER, M.G. (1968) 'A study of Sibawayhi's principles of grammatical analysis', unpublished PhD thesis, University of Oxford.

CARTER, M.G. (1972) 'Les Origines de la grammaire arabe', *Revue des Etudes Islamiques*, 49.

CARTER, M.G. (1973) 'An Arab grammarian of the eighth century', *Journal of the American Oriental Society*, 93.

CARTER, M.G. (1980) 'Sībawayhi and modern linguistics', *Histoire, Epistémologie, Langage*, II, 1.

CARTER, M.G. (1983) 'Language control as people control in Medieval Islam', *Al-Abḥāṯ*, 31.

CULIOLI, A. (1982) 'The role of metalinguistic representations in syntax', in *Proceedings of the Thirteenth International Congress of Linguists*. Tokyo.

FLEISCH, H. (1961) *Traité de philologie arabe*, vol. 1: *Préliminaires, phonétique, morphologie*, Beirut: Imprimerie Catholique.

GOLDENBERG, G. (1988) 'Subject and predicate in Arab grammatical tradition', *Zeitschrift des Deutschen Morgenländische Gesellschaft*, 138, 1.

GUILLAUME, G.· (1973) *Principes de linguistique théorique de Gustave Guillaume*, Paris: Klincksieck.

GUILLAUME, J.-P. (1986) 'Recherches sur la tradition grammaticale arabe', unpublished doctoral thesis, University of Paris-3.

GUILLAUME, J.-P. (1988) 'Le discours tout entier est nom, verbe et particule', *Langages*, 92.

HADJ-SALAH, A. (1971) 'La notion de syllabe et la théorie cinético-impulsionnelle des phonéticiens arabes', *Al-Lisāniyyāt*.

JAHN, G. (1895) *Sibawayhis Buch über die Grammatik*. Berlin.

KOULOUGHLI, D.E. (1986) 'Sur la structure interne des syllabes "lourdes" en arabe classique', *Revue Québécoise de Linguistique*, 16, 1.

KOULOUGHLI, D.E. (1987a) 'Fī mafhūmay al-taʿdiya wa-l-luzūm: ta'ammulāt naẓariyya ḥawla mas'ala xilāfiyya bayna l-naḥwiyyīn al-baṣriyyīn wa-l-kūfiyyīn. *Al-Lisāniyyāt*.

KOULOUGHLI, D.E. (1987b) 'Les Particules ont-elles un sens? (Autour d'une controverse dans la tradition grammaticale arabe.)', *Bulletin de Linguistique Appliquée et Générale*, 13, Université de Besançon.

LEVIN, A. (1981) 'The grammatical terms al-musnad, al-musnad 'ilayhi and al-'isnād', *Journal of the American Oriental Society*, 101.

MAHDI, M. (1970) 'Language and logic in Classical Islām', in *Logic in Classical Islamic Culture*, Wiesbaden: Von Grunebaum.

MARGOLIOUTH, N. (1905) 'The discussion between Abū Bišr Mattā and Abū Saʿīd al-Sīrāfī on the merits of logic and grammar', *Journal of the Royal Asiatic Society*.

MERX, A. (1889) *Historia artis grammaticae apud syros*, Leipzig.

MUBĀRAK, M. (1974) *Al-Naḥw al-ʿarabī*, Beyrut, Cairo.

ROBINS, R.H. (1967) *A short history of linguistics*, London and Harlow: Longmans Green.

TALMON, R. (1986) 'Who was the first Arab grammarian? A new approach to an old problem', *Journal of Arabic Linguistics*, 15.

TROUPEAU, G. (1976) *Lexique-index du 'Kitāb' de Sībawayh*, Paris: Klincksieck.

VERSTEEGH, C.H.M. (1977) *Greek elements in Arabic linguistic thinking*, Leiden: Brill.

WEIL, G. (1960) *ʿArūḍ. The Encyclopaedia of Islam*, 2nd edn, Leiden: Brill; Paris: Maisonneuve Max Besson.

INDEX RERUM

Note: numbers in **bold** refer to passages where the indexed notion is most thematic.

Active participle *see* Ism al-fā'il
Ambiguity: in syntactic analysis 61–2; in morphophonology 21, 85–6
Arabic writing system 93
Arabs, the: as reference speakers 18–19, 25–9, 80; speech of *see* Kalām al-'Arab
Aṣl: hard core of a category 51; primary form (morphology) 73, 78–92 *passim*; root (morphology) 74, 76; basic entity in a qiyās 26; *see also* far', qiyās
Aš'arite *see* Mu'tazilite–Aš'arite controversy
Axḏ al-luġa: classification of linguistic data 20
'Amal (syntactic government) 34–6, 38–40, **57–72**
'Āmil ma'nawī (abstract governing operator) 60; *see also* ibtidā', nominal sentence

Baṣran and Kūfan 'schools' 6–7, 69–71, 83
Binya aṣliyya (morphological structure) 74, 76

Class unity (principle of) 83, 88–9; *see also* phonological rules
Commentaries (grammatical) 14–15, 119
Consonant clusters 92–3
Criteriology (grammatical) 40–2

Ḍamīr mustatir ('masked' pronoun) 66
Ḍarā'ir al-ši'r (poetical constraints) 20
Ḍarūriyyāt al-fi'l (necessary elements of the verb) 68; *see also* verbal sentence

Faḍalāt (non-predicative elements of the sentence) 65, 66, 70–1; *see also* 'umad
Falsafa (Hellenic philosophical tradition) 8–9, 13–14, **104–9**
Far' (derived element of a qiyās) 26, 104; *see also* aṣl, qiyās
Fā'il ('doer', subject of a verb) 10–11, 45, 57, 67; *see also* verbal sentence

Glide-vowel sequences 21, **83–9**; *see also* istiṯqāl
Government (syntactic) *see* 'amal
Ǧumla (sentence) 44–7, **55–7**; *see also* kalām

Heaviness *see* istiṯqāl
Ḥaḏf (elision) 62–3, 82, 91–2, 127
Ḥadīṯ (authenticated report

concerning the Prophet's sayings and/or doings) 18, 101, 109

Ibtidā' (inchoation of a nominal sentence) 43, 46, 58, 60, 64, 69
Idġām (gemination, assimilation) 73, **90–1**, 94
Iḍāfa (annexion, status constructus) 55, 63, 127
Inna class particles 25, 53, 60, 65
Inšā' (performative predication) 56, 120, **130–1**; *see also* xabar
Islamic law 4, 18; *see also* uṣūl al-fiqh
Ism al-fā'il (active participle) 25, 52, 76, 79; *see also* verbo-nominal elements
Ism al-ğins (substantive noun) 52
Isnād (predication) 11, 43, 55–6, 65, **64–72**, 120, 123
Istiṯqāl (phonological 'heaviness') 21, 27–8, 80–92 *passim*; *see also* phonological rules
Iṣṭilāḥ (conventional origin of language) 110; *see also* origin of language, tawqīf
I'ğāz *see* Qur'an (inimitability of)
I'rāb (case and mood endings) 33, 50, **53–5**, 58, 70
'Ilal: speculative grammar, as opposed to uṣūl 10, **11–13**, 17; grammatical explanation 25, 27
'Ilm al-luġa (lexicography) 3, 4, 94
'Ilm al-'arūḍ (metrics) 3, **137–51**

Kalām al-'Arab (speech of the Arabs) 2–3, 9–10, 12–13, **18–22**, 41
Kalām (utterance) 40–1, 42–8, 55–7, 112, **121–5**
Kāna class auxiliary verbs 53, 65
Kūfan 'school' 11; *see also* Basran and Kufan 'schools'

Lafẓ (linguistic form) 9, 103, 110–11; *see also* ma'nā
Lexicography *see* 'ilm al-luġa
Logic (Aristotelian) 4, 9, 104–5; *see also* mimesis
Long vowels (status of) 99 n.3

Maṣdar (verbal noun) 47, 52, 74, 76; *see also* verbo-nominal elements
Ma'nā (plur. ma'ānī, meaning) 9, 54, 73, 74, 76, 98 n.1 and 2, 103, 115; ma'ānī l-ši'r (poetical themes) 103, 106; ma'ānī l-naḥw (syntactico-semantical categories) 116; linguistic vs. 'assentive' 112–13; noun-like vs. particle-like 111–12; proper vs. figurative 111, 118, **135–6**; primary vs. secondary 122, 130; relational 112
Metalinguistic vs. linguistic usage 32, 36–8, 58–9
Metre **137–41**
Mimesis (Aristotelian) 105, 108
Modal particles (inna class) 25, 53, 60, 65
Mubtada' (theme of a nominal sentence) 11, 35, 43, 57, 60, 69
Muḥākāt wa-taxyīl (imitation and suggestion) *see* mimêsis
Musnad (predicate) *see* isnād
Musnad ilay-hi (predicand) *see* isnād
Muṭṭarid (regular fact) 20
Mu'tazilite school 58, 135; Mu'tazilite–Aš'arite controversy 113–16

Naql al-luġa (authentification of linguistic data) 18
Nawāsix al-ibtidā' (abrogators of ibtidā') 65
Naẓm (textual organization) 115–17
Nā'ib fā'il (subject surrogate) *see* verbal sentence (passive), ḍarūriyyāt al-fi'l
Nominal sentence 58, 64–5, 68–72

Organization of grammar 5–6, 10–11, 33
Origin of language 29–30, 110–12

Performative predication *see* inšā'
Philology 3, 5
Phonological rules (application of) 21, 86, 88–9
Poetry (Arabic) 2–3, 18, 20, 100–4; *see also* ma'ānī l-ši'r, metre, ḍarā'ir al-ši'r, sariqa
Pragmatics 103, 113, 119, 121–2, 129; *see also* situation of communication
Predication *see* isnād
Production of speech sounds 97–8
Prosody 97

Qayd ('constraint') 123–4
Qirā'āt (variant readings of the Qur'ān) *see* Qur'ān (recension of)
Qiyās: heuristic reasoning 2, **22–6**, 51, 78, 88, 109; rational elaboration 6, 26; *see also* samā'
Qur'ān 18, 109, 130–6 *passim*; exegesis of 5, 51, 62, 118; inimitability of 113–17; recensions of 2, 96; ritual recitation of *see* taǧwīd

Samā' (transmitted data) 6, 26
Sariqa (poetical plagiarism) 103
Sentence *see* ǧumla
Situation of communication 108, 121, 126, 130; *see also* pragmatics
Stoic grammar 4
Subject *see* fā'il
Syllables (status of) 95, 137, 143, 150
Synchrony vs. diachrony 29, 78
Šāḏḏ ('irregular' data) 20

Tadāxul al-luǧāt (commingling of dialectal forms) 22
Taǧwīd (ritual recitation of the Qur'ān) 93, **96–7**
Taqdīm wa-ta'xīr (anteposition and postposition) 36, 39, 57, 128; *see also* word order
Taqdīr (abstract representation) 20, 60, **62–3**
Taqyīd (constraining) 124, 127–8; *see also* qayd
Tarāfu' (reciprocal assignment of the nominative) 69–72
Tawābi' (dependencies of a noun phrase) 58
Tawqīf (origin of language by decree of God) 110
Ṭalab (rogative predication) 56, 107

Unity of paradigm *see* phonological rules
Uṣūl (fundaments): descriptive grammar 10–11; uṣūl al-fiqh (fundaments of jurisprudence) 51, 100, **109–13**; uṣūl al-naḥw (fundaments of grammar) 17, 19
Utterance *see* kalām
'Umad (predicative elements of the sentence) 65, 70–1; *see also* faḍalāt

Verb: as a complex unit 46–7, 66–7, 74, 112; complements of 67–8; government of 59, 64
Verbal sentence 57, **64–8**; passive 10, 67–8
Verbo-nominals 52–3, 58–9, 66

Watid (stable metrical element) 137–50 *passim*
Wazn (morphological pattern) 76–8
Word order 35–6, 65–6, 107, 132; *see also* taqdīm wa-ta'xīr

Xabar: constative predication 56, 107, 120, **128–30**; predicate of a nominal sentence 11, 43, 44

Ẓanna class cognitive verbs 34–40, 65
Ẓurūf (circumstants) 52, 67, 125–6

INDEX NOMINUM

Abū Hāšim al-Ǧubbā'ī 115
Abū Mūsā al-Murdār 113
Abū l-Aswad al-Du'alī 1
Abū l-Barakāt al-Anbārī 17, 59
Abū ʻAlī al-Fārisī 28, 83
Aristotle 104, 107, 108, 128
Asmaʻī (al-) 101
Astarābā<u>d</u>ī (al-) 11, 16, 56, **68–72**, 81, 88, 92
Ašmūnī (al-) 16
Avicenna *see* Ibn Sīnā
Axfaš al-Awsaṭ (al-) 5
ʻAbd Allāh ibn Abī Isḥāq 1
ʻAbd al-Ǧabbār (the Qāḍī-) 115–16
ʻAbd al-Malik ibn Marwān 3, 93
ʻAbd al-Qāhir al-Ǧurǧānī 116–17, 118, 120, **123–4**, 128
ʻAlī ibn Abī Ṭālib 1

Bāqillānī (al-) 114

Fārābī (al-) 10, 105, 106
Farrā' (al-) 5, 71

Ǧāḥiẓ (al-) **103**, 107, 113, 129
Ǧumaḥī (al-) **101–2**
Ǧurǧānī (ʻAbd al-Qāhir al-) *see* ʻAbd al-Qāhir al-Ǧurǧānī
Ḡazālī (al-) 109

Hišām ibn Muʻāwiya 71
Ḥaǧǧāǧ ibn Yūsuf (al-) 93
Ḥāzim al-Qarṭaǧannī 108–9

Ibn al-Muʻtazz 104
Ibn ʻAqīl 16
Ibn al-Sarrāǧ 4, **10–11**, 14, 55, 67, 69
Ibn Ǧinnī **11–13**, 15, 17, **26–30**, 56, 78–90 *passim*, 92, 96
Ibn Hišām 14, 15, 50, 62
Ibn Maḍā' 58
Ibn Mālik 15
Ibn Qutayba 103–4, 107
Ibn Sīnā (Avicenna) **97–8**, 105
Ibn Yaʻīš 15, 16, 52, 55–6, 68, 78–9, 81, 82–92 *passim*
Ibn ʻUṣfūr 73, 83
Isḥāq ibn Wahb **107–8**

Kisā'ī (al-) 71

Mubarrad (al-) 5, 7, 8, 21, 24, 56

Naẓẓām (al-) 113, 129

Qazwīnī (al-) **119–20**, 128
Qudāma ibn Ǧaʻfar **105–8**

Rummānī (al-) 15, 114

Sakkākī (al-) **118–19**
Sībawayhi 1, 4–5, 12, **31–48**, 50, 55, 56, 94
Sīrāfī (al-) 13, 14
Suyūṭī (al-) 16–17
Šāfiʻī (al-) 109

Ṯa'lab 7–8, 104, 107

Xalīl (al-) 4, 26, 90, **93–4**, 141
Xaṭṭābī (al-) **113–14**

Zaǧǧāǧī (al-) 11, 17, **25–6**, 55, 58
Zamaxšarī (al-) 56, **68**, 118